The Archaeology of Clothing and Bodily Adornment in Colonial America

THE AMERICAN EXPERIENCE IN ARCHAEOLOGICAL PERSPECTIVE

UNIVERSITY PRESS OF FLORIDA

Florida A&M University, Tallahassee
Florida Atlantic University, Boca Raton
Florida Gulf Coast University, Ft. Myers
Florida International University, Miami
Florida State University, Tallahassee
New College of Florida, Sarasota
University of Central Florida, Orlando
University of Florida, Gainesville
University of North Florida, Jacksonville
University of South Florida, Tampa
University of West Florida, Pensacola

THE AMERICAN EXPERIENCE IN ARCHAEOLOGICAL PERSPECTIVE
Edited by Michael S. Nassaney

The books in this series explore an event, process, setting, or institution that was significant in the formative experience of contemporary America. Each volume will frame the topic beyond an individual site and attempt to give the reader a flavor of the theoretical, methodological, and substantive issues that researchers face in their examination of that topic or theme. These books will be comprehensive overviews that will allow serious students and scholars to get a good sense of contemporary and past inquiries on a broad theme in American history and culture.

The Archaeology of Collective Action, by Dean J. Saitta (2007)
The Archaeology of Institutional Confinement, by Eleanor Conlin Casella (2007)
The Archaeology of Race and Racialization in Historic America, by Charles E. Orser Jr. (2007)
The Archaeology of North American Farmsteads, by Mark D. Groover (2008)
The Archaeology of Alcohol and Drinking, by Frederick H. Smith (2008)
The Archaeology of American Labor and Working-Class Life, by Paul A. Shackel (2009)
The Archaeology of Clothing and Bodily Adornment in Colonial America, by Diana DiPaolo
     Loren (2010)

~ ❀ ~

The Archaeology of Clothing
and Bodily Adornment
in Colonial America

~ ❀ ~

Diana DiPaolo Loren

Foreword by Michael S. Nassaney

University Press of Florida
Gainesville · Tallahassee · Tampa · Boca Raton
Pensacola · Orlando · Miami · Jacksonville · Ft. Myers · Sarasota

First cloth printing, 2010
First paperback printing, 2011

Library of Congress Cataloging-in-Publication Data
Loren, Diana DiPaolo.
The archaeology of clothing and bodily adornment in colonial America / Diana
DiPaolo Loren, foreword by Michael S. Nassaney.
p. cm.—(The American experience in archaeological perspective)
Includes bibliographical references and index.
ISBN 978-0-8130-3501-7 (alk. paper); ISBN 978-0-8130-3803-2 (pbk)
1. Clothing and dress—United States—History—17th century. 2. Dress accessories—
United States—History—17th century. 3. Clothing and dress—United States—
History—18th century. 4. Dress accessories—United States—History—18th century.
5. Excavations (Archaeology)—United States. 6. United States—History—Colonial
period, ca. 1600–1775 7. United States—Social life and customs—To 1775.
8. United States—Antiquities. I. Nassaney, Michael S. II. Title.
GT607.L67 2010
391.00973—dc22   2010016627

The University Press of Florida is the scholarly publishing agency for the State University System of Florida, comprising Florida A&M University, Florida Atlantic University, Florida Gulf Coast University, Florida International University, Florida State University, New College of Florida, University of Central Florida, University of Florida, University of North Florida, University of South Florida, and University of West Florida.

University Press of Florida
15 Northwest 15th Street
Gainesville, FL 32611-2079
http://www.upf.com

To my husband

Contents

Figures

Foreword

Postcolonial scholarship continues to examine the constitution of society and find utility in the lens of identity. Archaeologists and other social scientists concerned with the social world investigate how individuals and collectivities are distinguished in their relationships with others. Many hold that social identities—a composite of the socially sanctioned roles that individuals enact as members of a group—are never created in isolation; they are the outcomes of interactions. Under conditions of colonial entanglements in the Americas and elsewhere, identities were conceived as fluid and malleable, under negotiation, and open to manipulation. Archaeologists can explore the forms that these new identities took in colonial America because identity was constructed and expressed through the material world.

In *The Archaeology of Clothing and Bodily Adornment in Colonial America*, Diana DiPaolo Loren examines the apparel and objects that people employed to enclose and attach to their bodies to interrogate the American experience. Though limited in number due to curation, perishability, and other factors, sartorial artifacts are among the remains that were lost, abandoned, or discarded at most archaeological sites. Such objects were used to construct a physical appearance and convey information about status, occupation, ethnicity, religion, and sexual preference. Consumers acquired clothing and adornment through an active selection process and employed them as visual enhancements to express personhood that literally became parts of their bodies. Beads, bracelets, buckles, and buttons are just a few objects that were powerful visual metaphors in the marking of personal and collective identities, and they reveal the choices that people made in daily life in colonial America. The analysis of sartorial expression can contribute to the study of colonial society in which material culture was manipulated to signal a range of messages about not only personal identity but also relations to the homeland and the new social opportunities that colonial life engendered.

Objects of clothing—most notably Yugoslavian hats—were instrumental in the archaeological literature of the 1970s that first posited that style had function. Rather than being merely epiphenomenal, style communicated information to casual observers provided they could decode the messages. Unlike auditory media, messages broadcast through material culture were enduring and could be received in the absence of the emitter. Clothing and adornment are ideal media for exchanging stylistic information, and they provide insight into social strategies of identity formation.

Fashion choices were constrained by sumptuary laws in seventeenth- and eighteenth-century America that sought to maintain social boundaries of class, race, and ethnicity. Yet people crafted fashions according to practicality, social context, and daily experience, creating a new world of clothing possibilities that rubbed against the grain of the legal restrictions colonists faced and were expected to follow. As archaeology has shown repeatedly, practice confronted principles, particularly among those segments of the population who lived "along the margins of historical narratives." By viewing clothing at the intersection of multiple lines of evidence—archaeological, documentary, ethnographic, and pictorial—Loren challenges us to see beyond the essential identity ascribed to an object at the time of its production based upon its intended function and to envision the symbolic meanings and values that artifacts acquire through use. She also urges us to look beyond the static categories that analysts use to organize collections by raw material and function. The sources accessible to the historical archaeologist expose the varying ways and unique combinations of clothing styles that colonials used to express their place in society.

The population of the eighteenth-century site of Fort St. Joseph in the western Great Lakes included diverse occupants who varied by age, status, ethnicity, gender, and religious affiliation, all of whom had the potential to use material objects to express personal identities under unstable social and political conditions. In this historical context, the active manipulation of items of clothing and adornment was commonplace, and seemingly mundane items were poignant markers of tensions and contradictions. As an example, imported glass beads, buttons, and brooches were likely worn in combination with domestically produced shell beads and tinkling cones by both Native Americans and the French who donned shared, hybrid-style clothing that expressed their close alliance with Native peoples in opposition to the English and the conventions of the Crown. However, some segments of the population may have used forms of imported personal adornment such as glass-inset sleeve buttons, decorative buckles, and ornate finger rings to identify with Old World notions of status, patriarchy, loyalty, and civility, suggesting the multilayered and multivocal meanings of material mediations of the self.

As Loren notes, the archaeological record is a key component of interpreting the colonial past because all colonial relations were constituted with material culture. Indeed, all social relations are created and reproduced through the (albeit contextually situated) material world. Clothing and adornment are particularly significant in this regard because of their role in the presentation of the self. Not surprisingly, the approach advocated here to the colonial world has application to the analysis of more recent fashion trends. Such studies will serve to extend our understanding of the role of apparel and other accoutrements in the American experience. Witness the evolution of the T-shirt since the mid-twentieth century: each successive generation has employed this former undergarment in emblematic fashion to distinguish itself from its predecessors and make a political statement. Suffice it to say that clothing and bodily adornment have long been woven into the fabric of the American experience and that as long as people are losing buttons archaeology will have a contribution to make in understanding this dimension of our collective pasts.

Michael S. Nassaney
Series Editor

A Short Preface and
Some Acknowledgements

I begin this book with a backward glance. Growing up in Philadelphia and having seen my fair share of historical reenactments (especially at the Bicentennial Celebration), I never questioned colonial garb. When I started in archaeology, the very first item I excavated was an artifact of personal adornment (a common copper-alloy shoe buckle) from the Rittenhouse-Town site in Fairmount Park, Philadelphia. Perhaps my interest in the archaeology of colonial clothing and adornment started there, leading me on a certain trajectory that led me to write a book on the subject.

But truthfully, my sincere interest in the subject of dress, clothing, and adornment began when looking at the artifacts from Presidio Los Adaes, the subject of my doctoral dissertation. I was fascinated with the buttons, buckles, and other small finds recovered from the site and knew that those artifacts could lead me toward an understanding of constructions of identity in the colonial period. But archaeological writings on clothing and adornment related to constructions of colonial identity were few and far between at the time, as most sources about small finds dealt with identifying and categorizing recovered objects rather than with interpreting them. Through my work on this collection, I grew to know the colonial world as much more richly and deeply textured than I had previously realized, populated by peoples in various dress. And I soon found inspiration and validation in the work of Mary Beaudry, Kent Lightfoot, Kathleen Deagan, Joan Comaroff, Martin Hall, and Ann Stoler: scholars who tackle issues of pluralism, identity, and bodily dress and comportment.

Now, years later, I am grateful to be among a cohort of archaeologists who, like myself, seek to understand how and why colonial peoples dressed in the ways that they did. So, when I was asked to write a short volume on colonial clothing and adornment through the lens of historical archaeology, I was eager to add my voice to the chorus and write a bit more on the subject. Many thanks are given to Michael Nassaney for allowing me to pursue this topic that occupies much of my thoughts (both academic and otherwise) in a volume for his excellent series.

The Peabody Museum of Archaeology and Ethnology at Harvard University is home to one of the largest and oldest collections of material culture in the Western Hemisphere and has provided me with many sources of inspiration. More importantly, I derive excellent support from my colleagues there, especially William Fash, Lisa Barbash, Julie Brown, Trish Capone, Amy Cay, Catherine Ceseaux, Jessica Ganong, Sandra Dong, Viva Fisher, Susan Haskell, Christina Hodge, Steven Leblanc, Castle McLaughlin, David Schafer, and Rubie Watson. Jessica Ganong helped me organize the images for the book and was patient with me throughout the process. Ying to my curatorial yang, Trish Capone is also my guide on NAGPRA work at the museum. I am in awe of her leadership, thoughtfulness, and graciousness in this important work as well as so many other matters. I am also in sincere debt to Christina Hodge, whose opinion, wit, and sage advice have helped me throughout this process and in our collaborative work at the museum. Susan Haskell is a wealth of knowledge about the museum collections and I am thankful that she shares her knowledge with me. Sandra Dong brought the Tlingit coat featured in Chapter 4 to the attention of the museum as part of her ongoing research. She also provided identification of the Chinese coins, and I thank her for allowing me to include that information here. Viva Fisher, co-author and dear friend, shared the Edith Wharton quote used in Chapter 6.

William Fash, Trish Capone, Christina Hodge, Dylan Clark, Molly Fierer-Donaldson, Emily Pierce, and Michele Koons are my collaborators on the Harvard Yard Archaeology Project (HYAP). As always, I am thankful of their partnership and support on this program and for their insight, knowledge, and humor about many other things academic, museum, and otherwise. I have also benefited from the diligent research by undergraduate and graduate students on the project, especially Nathaniel Amdur-Clark, Danielle Charlap, Sakura Christmas, Trevor Johnson, Rachel Sayet, and Sally Stephens. HYAP's work on the seventeenth-century Harvard Indian College and my own work on the colonial body and dress have benefited from discussions with many members of the Harvard University Native

American Program, including Carmen Lopez, Jackie Old Coyote, Jonella Larson, Desireé Martinez, Judy Kertz, Troy Monserrat-Gonzales, and Sharri Clark, as well as the members of Native Americans at Harvard College, especially Caitlin Young and Maggie Spivey.

My research on the archaeology of clothing and adornment has been enhanced by the museum's work with many Native groups that honor us with their presence and kindly share with us their knowledge. I extend my gratitude to all of these visitors and especially to Rose Berens and Vern Adams from the Bois Forte Band of Chippewa Indians, who helped me to see glass beads, quite literally, in a new light.

I am thankful to be part of an academic community where there are many fine scholars and colleagues whose own work on clothing and adornment consistently inspires me: Mary Beaudry, Kathleen Deagan, Viva Fisher, Rosemary Joyce, Rob Mann, Lynn Meskell, Ruth Phillips, Nan Rothschild, Pat Rubertone, Ann Stahl, Carolyn White, and Barb Voss are among them and I am grateful for their scholarship, comments, and insights. My writings on the colonial period continue to be inspired by my conversations with some truly outstanding scholars, including Lisa Brooks, Charlie Cobb, Amy Groleau, Siobhan Hart, Kent Lightfoot, Melinda Maynor Lowery, Tim Pauketat, Steve Silliman, and Giovanna Vitelli. Michael Nassaney and two anonymous reviewers provided valuable critiques to this manuscript. I thank John Byram, Marthe Walters, and Kate Babbitt of the University Press of Florida for their help and patience while shepherding me through the process of writing this book.

In recent years, I had the opportunity to teach two courses related to my interests. In Spring 2006, I taught a course on the ancient body at Brown University. Discussions with students in that course inspired many of the topics I discuss in this volume. In Fall 2007, I taught a graduate seminar on materiality and museum practice at the University of Massachusetts, Boston. Many thanks to the students in that class who challenged my ideas and brought their own to the table each week, and many thanks to Steve Silliman and Steve Mrozowski for the opportunity to teach the class.

It is interesting to look back to my life as a teenager and to see my life then expressed in my writings today. During my early teen years, I was employed at a funky retail clothing store in a suburb of Philadelphia. There I worked with an indescribable group of women who taught me all about fashion in just a few short years and made an indelible impression on my style. My mother was one of my co-workers at that job. For as long as I can remember, my mother has taught me about fashion. I have no greater teacher about clothing and adornment than the woman who has always inspired me to dress my best.

Finally, I get unfailing support, laughter, and joy from my beautiful family: my amazing husband and our fantastic little Lily. Lewis has supported me from art school into graduate school and then onto Cambridge. He is a never-ending source of gut-ripping laughter. It is his ink that inspired the inclusion of tattooing in Chapter 3. And he inspires me in so many other ways. Thank you, Lewis, for everything.

D. D. L.

1

~ ✿ ~

Clothing and Adornment
in Colonial North America

I say, beware of all enterprises that require new clothes,
and not rather a wearer of new clothes.
—Henry David Thoreau

In this book, I consider the dress, clothing, and adornment of peoples living in seventeenth- and eighteenth-century North America through the lens of historical archaeology, aided by ethnographic, historical, and visual sources. The archaeological record provides us with a narrow view of clothing and adornment: a button from a cloak or a buckle from a shoe is usually all that remains from an item or garment. We can learn more of the entire item or garment through other sources: paintings, account books, and ethnographic collections. Each of these sources provides a slightly different (and often biased) view of colonial dress. But at their intersection, we have the potential to understand how the tiny button recovered from an eighteenth-century privy was attached to clothing, how the person dressed in that fashion moved through a somewhat unstable colonial world, and, more importantly, how dress in colonial America mattered.

One need only reference the crimson "A" worn by Hester Prynne in Nathaniel Hawthorne's *The Scarlet Letter* to imagine the impact of clothing and adornment in the colonies. During the colonial period, clothing was important not only for Puritans living in New England but also for Native Americans, Europeans, Africans, and peoples of multiethnic ancestry occupying settlements and towns throughout North America. Dress was a social medium. The color, fabric, and fit of clothing in combination with adornments, posture, and manners conveyed information about status, occupation, religious beliefs, and even sexual preferences of the clothed and adorned person (see Anderson 2005; Entwistle 2000; Richardson 2004). Clothing and adornment is therefore important not only for its utility but also for its expressive properties and the ability of the wearer to manipulate properties embodied through dress (Shannon 1996:17).

During the seventeenth and eighteenth centuries, European production of clothing, cloth, and adornment was blossoming, tied to a growing global economy (Baumgarten 2002). New fabrics, buttons, beads, shoes, and shirts were just some of the items available to peoples living in North America. Clothing, which was still largely constructed by hand, was made both within and outside North America. Quite literally, a new world of clothing (and by extension fashion) was available to communities outside Europe (Breen 1993). During these centuries, English, Spanish, Dutch, French, and Russian colonies in North America were populated by Europeans, Africans, Native Americans, and individuals of multiethnic ancestry. Each of these groups had different dressing traditions. Because of the complex makeup of peoples inhabiting North America and the interest of colonial officials in controlling this population, ideas, rules, and restrictions about the ways that certain people were to dress were abundant. Not everyone could take

1.1. *The Bermuda Group (Dean Berkeley and His Entourage),* painting by John Smibert, 1729. Courtesy of Yale University Art Gallery.

1.2. *Desseins de Sauvages de Plusieurs Nations,* watercolor by Alexandre de Batz, ca. 1734. Courtesy of President and Fellows of Harvard College, Peabody Museum of Archaeology and Ethnology, 41-72-10/20.

advantage of new fashions or dress in the ways they wished. Despite such limitations (or attempted limitations), colonial peoples dressed in ways that strained against the seams of colonial rule.

The image that clothing and adornment in colonial America conjures in the minds of many is the one found at historical reenactment sites such as colonial Williamsburg: men wearing frock coats and knee breeches, their heads covered by powdered wigs and tricorn hats (Figure 1.1). These images of colonial elites are tempered by other depictions of the peoples and fashions that populated colonial North America. A 1734 watercolor by Alexandre de Batz that illustrates different Native and African peoples living in French colonial Louisiana was drawn just five years after John Smibert's painting of Dean Berkeley and his entourage (Figure 1.2). The style and medium of the two images are quite different, but generally speaking their subject is the same: colonial peoples. The individuals depicted in these images were from different ethnic and racial backgrounds, occupied different physical spaces in the colonial world, and wore different styles of clothing and adornment. These images illustrate that there was no single fashion or preferred style of dressing for the many peoples who lived in North

America; their dress was as diverse as the physical and social spaces they occupied. What these images fail to capture is the ingenuity and creativity of colonial dress—how different groups of people living together in communities throughout North America consciously clothed and adorned their bodies in specific ways to create a sense of self and present that self in their worlds. Jean Comaroff (1996:19) notes that dress was "a privileged means for constructing new forms of value, personhood, and history on the colonial frontier." Although her writing focuses on colonial South Africa, Comaroff's words have relevance for colonial North America. While no one fashion typified colonial life, what was integral to the American colonial experience was that people created specific fashions of clothing and adornment appropriate to their context and their daily experiences (see Shannon 1996; St. George 2000).

In colonial North America, individuals from many ethnic groups transformed clothing traditions through processes of cultural exchange. The strategies they used suggest a pattern of dressing in colonial North America that is best characterized as a patchwork, a mixture of local and imported, Native and non-Native, handmade and manufactured. The strategy of combining locally made and imported goods created a new language of appearance that individuals used to communicate self and identity in an often-contentious colonial world (Comaroff 1996; Shannon 1996:19). In this book, I explore the active manipulation of the material culture of clothing and adornment by people in English, Dutch, French, and Spanish colonies. I examine how peoples in these different contexts combined objects of clothing and adornment in unique ways to dress themselves in distinct fashions.

While historical and visual accounts of the colonial past are informative about the ways various peoples dressed (and these sources are used almost exclusively in period reenactments), they provide only one perspective. This perspective is inherently biased toward elite European men and offers little surviving information about the other peoples who occupied colonial landscapes. When we look to historical sources to visually recreate past life, we must take care not to do so at the expense of the women, children, Africans, Native Americans, and servants who lived in the margins of historical narratives. That historical archaeology is best suited to provide detailed information about the daily practices of colonial peoples that takes into account ethnicity, gender, or race is a well-established tenet of the discipline (for just a few examples, see Beaudry 1998; Deagan 1988; Hall 1992, 2000; Orser 2007).

When we focus our gaze on American history, we seek to visualize the characters in that past. While paintings, illustrations, woodcuts, and historical texts provide some description primarily about the dress of elite male individuals, we are left to imagine the dress of others, especially those overlooked in historical documents. This is where historical archaeology can broaden and (at times) challenge popular and academic representations of the clothing and adornment of colonial peoples.

Archaeologists study the residue of people's lives that has been left behind: the objects lost or discarded in daily activities or purposefully placed with a loved one at the time of burial. As an historical archaeologist, the category of material culture that seems to occupy my time and interest is small finds: those buttons, buckles, jewelry, fabric, and beads found on archaeological sites that are the remnants of pieces of clothing and adornment. The fact that we find these objects in a variety of contexts tells us much about who wore what and how they wore it. During the colonial period, numerous goods manufactured in Europe—items such as textiles, buttons, and glass beads—were shipped to North America in bulk lots. The movement of these goods to colonial communities along with sumptuary laws (official ideals of how colonial peoples were to dress) were meant to set the fashion and tastes for colonial populations. Imperial leaders had a certain vision of dress for their populations and went to great lengths to make sure that those visions were realized (Breen 1993).

Once ships arrived in the colonies, goods were sent to merchants and warehouses from which colonial people could outfit their wardrobes. Because of this global market, some of the same items used in practices of dressing are found at very different types of sites in the French, English, Dutch and Spanish colonies of North America. For example, in the eighteenth century, metal sleeve buttons manufactured in England were shipped across the Atlantic to adorn the clothes of Wampanoag, African, and English peoples living in New England and the mid-Atlantic. As a result, the same style of sleeve buttons found in the basement of the first college building in North America was also found buried with an African man in New York. In this case and many others, while the same item of clothing and adornment may have been found in different contexts, it was mobilized in distinct ways by colonial peoples to create different fashions in the colonies that led to multifaceted and multilayered visions of dress in the American experience.

This book in not intended as a sourcebook for identifying objects of clothing and adornment in the archaeological record. Several excellent sourcebooks of this kind have already been published (e.g., Deagan 2002; Noël Hume 1969; White 2005). My intent in this book is to problematize and unpack notions of colonial clothing and adornment by examining a variety of classes of data that are available to the historical archaeologist: archaeological, ethnographic, historical, and visual.

The examples of clothing and adornment discussed in this book focus on how people manipulated and combined objects that were manufactured both locally and abroad. I draw from the sources I just mentioned—archaeological, ethnographic, historical, and visual—to illustrate some of the unique combinations of clothing and adornment found throughout colonial North America. I rely heavily on collections of colonial material housed within the Peabody Museum of Archaeology and Ethnology at Harvard University. As the oldest museum of archaeology and ethnology in the western hemisphere, the museum is steward to very early ethnographic collections from North America as well as collections from numerous archaeological investigations. In addition to these museum collections, I compare similar material culture from other colonial contexts, relying on anthropological and archaeological scholarship (Figure 1.3).

One of the great advantages of interdisciplinary research is that scholars can discover disjunctures between sources and silences that illuminate points of contention and anxiety about colonial policies and practices (Hall 1992, 2004; Loren and Baram 2007; Stahl 1993). For example, when we direct our attention to material culture alone, we must be aware of biases in categorization and interpretation. Emphasizing one category in isolation—for example, the glass bead over the beaded garment—may limit what we can say about how identity was constituted using material culture. What can we know of the lives and struggles of people from an investigation of artifact assemblages that at first glance seem to contain unlikely and dissonant combinations of different categories of material culture? The answer lies in comparison—not only comparing the artifacts present in the assemblage but also comparing the artifacts we have with those that are not present. We must also look at the ways that the remnants of daily practices are or are not represented in historical, visual, and ethnographic material.

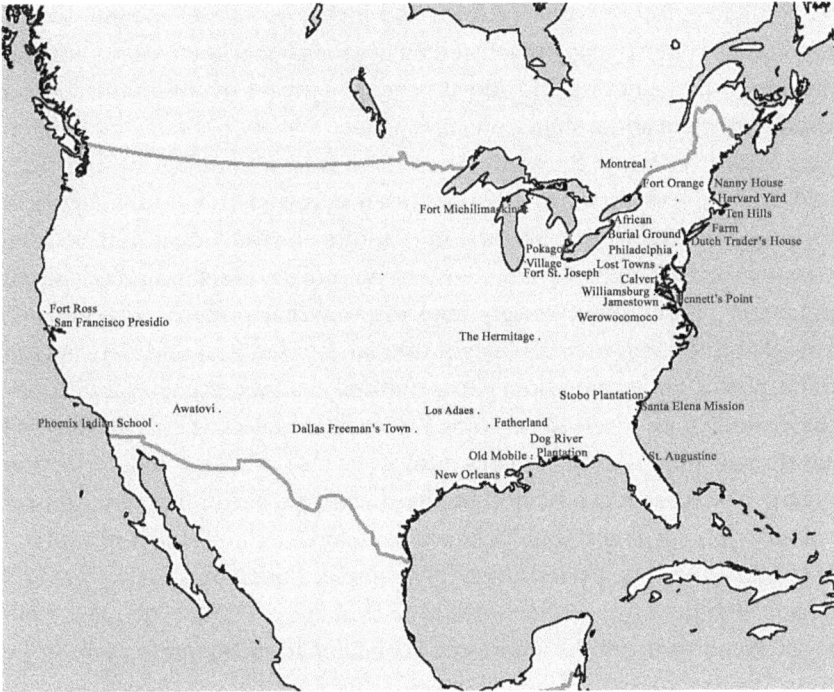

1.3. Archaeological sites mentioned in this book.

Not every example of clothing and adornment found in colonial contexts is examined in this book. Rather, I spotlight a few examples of specific kinds of clothing and adornment that have been recovered from multiple colonial contexts, lingering on those that best illustrate how a simple button, for example, can take on a multitude of meanings when worn by different colonial peoples. The purpose of my approach is to stimulate ideas about the ways that small things that have been forgotten about clothing and adornment provide an entry point into the thought worlds and practices of colonial men, women, and children of varying ethnic backgrounds. These clothing styles comprise the fabric of the American experience.

Interpreting the Clothed and Adorned Colonial Body

Theoretical approaches to dress, clothing, and fashion have long been discussed within the fields of history, art history, and visual studies. These approaches garnered attention within anthropology in the 1950s and 1960s, becoming popular in the 1990s through the work of Joanne B. Eicher and

Mary Ellen Roach-Higgins (Barnes and Eicher 1993; Eicher 1999; Eicher and Roach-Higgins 1992; Roach and Eicher 1965, 1973). Such works amplify the notion that clothing and adornment are a means of communication: a visual statement about status, prestige, gender, society, politics, and religion (see Anderson 2005; Entwistle 2000; Richardson 2004). Clothing faces both inward and outward, a notion Terence Turner (1993 [1980]) evoked when he coined the term "social skin." Culture, the individual, and clothing are inextricably linked, as there is often no more powerful, individualized statement of and about society than the way that someone dresses. Just a single button can provide insight into social identities and networks of trade, power, and production. Cross-cultural analysis reveals that in all societies bodies are "dressed" in some way and that everywhere clothing and adornment play "symbolic, communicative and aesthetic roles" (Wilson 1995:3). For these reasons, clothing has been a powerful topic for anthropologists, archaeologists, and scholars of material culture studying a variety of cultures and time periods (see, for example, Anderson 2005; Eicher and Roach-Higgins 1992; Eicher 1995; Goodwin 1999; Greenblatt 1984; Neill 2000; Richardson and Kroeber 1952; Schneider 2006; Shannon 1996; Stoler 2001; Weiner 1985; Weiner and Schneider 1989).

Historical archaeologists have long been mindful of the need to identify and categorize artifacts of clothing and adornment. There are deep traditions of interpreting objects of clothing and adornment at colonial sites such as Williamsburg, Fort Ross, Old Mobile, and the Spanish mission settlements of Florida (Baumgarten 2002; Deagan 2002; Lightfoot 1995; Quimby 1966; Waselkov 1992). Classic volumes within the discipline, such as Ivor Noël Hume's *A Guide to the Artifacts of Colonial America* (1969), are devoted to processes for identifying, classifying, and dating historical artifacts that are crucial to interpretive strategies (see also Emery and Fiske 1985). Scholars have also examined the manufacture, consumption patterns, and trade patterns related to the material culture of clothing and adornment (see, for example, Claassen 1994; Hamell 1983).

This material culture is commonly analyzed through the lenses of ethnicity, gender, and sexuality, with increasing emphasis being placed on the intersection of issues of materiality and embodiment (e.g., Comaroff 1996; Eicher 1999; Eicher and Roach-Higgins 1992:12; Greenblatt 1984; Voss 2008b; Weiner 1985; Weiner and Schneider 1989; see also Schneider 2006). Hansen (2003) outlines the growing interest in clothing within anthropology over the past two decades, pointing to book series such as Berg

Publishers' Dress, Body, and Culture series as examples of this trend. Yet in the absence of information related to gender, age, or ethnicity, a single article of clothing is usually interpreted along rather conservative lines, influenced by existing stereotypes or knowledge claims.

Dress is more than a surface phenomenon. Clothing and adornment do not just live on the exterior of one's body. How a person dresses, the sense of self that a person wishes to embody, is part of his or her bodily experience. Social archaeology—an exploration of the intersection of people and material culture—is necessary if we are to understand an individual's bodily experience with and in the colonial world (see Goodwin 1999; Gosden and Knowles 2001; Joyce 1998, 2005; Loren 2001a, 2001b, 2007a; Meskell 2002, 2004; Nassaney 2004). Broadly stated, social archaeology "conceptualized as an archaeology of social being can be located at the intersections of temporality, spatiality and materiality" (Pruecel and Meskell 2004:3). Within social archaeology, the body as a social and physical being has become more prominent. At the intersection of time, space, and the material, it is through the body that a person experiences the world, forms a sense of self and identity, and mediates social exchanges and social constructions of race, gender, power, and age (Butler 1990; Merleau-Ponty 1989; for further discussion of these concepts see Calefato 2004; Colchester 2003; DeMarrais et al. 2004; Entwistle and Wilson 2001; Gosden and Knowles 2001; Joyce 1998, 2005; Meskell 2004; Miller 2005; Thomas 1991; Voss 2008a).

In this book I investigate some of the ways that colonial peoples chose to express their bodies and identities through clothing and adornment. The body is at the core of this analysis. More than simply a mannequin for clothes, people's bodies were at the center of most colonial discussions of self and other. European racialization of Native and African bodies was in full swing by the mid-seventeenth century; most Europeans, regardless of their social status, claimed moral, bodily, and cultural superiority over these groups (Chaplin 2003:9, 14; Orser 2007). The body was the area where sexual, racial, and cultural differences were played out, making it possible for various peoples to visually understand and portray notions of comportment, nature, culture, intention, religious preference, and economic and social status (Deagan 2002; Loren 2001b, 2007a, 2007b).

Dress as a material expression of self was subject to change and innovation in relation to specific colonial contexts. The notion of "one costume, one culture" must be discarded if we seek to understand the diversity of clothing and identities in North American history. In this book, I ground my discussions in current theoretical perspectives on embodiment and materiality, which makes possible a discussion of how objects of clothing and adornment were an integral part of people's daily lives and how colonial identities were constituted through the active manipulation of material culture.

The Lives of Clothing and Objects of Adornment

This book explores the clothed and adorned body in colonial North America through the lens of historical archaeology. To bring out the ways that people actively manipulated clothing and adornment, we must interrogate the context in which objects of clothing and adornment were entangled with the lives of the people who created and wore them. As numerous examples from the archaeological, ethnographic, documentary, and visual records suggest, a tension often existed between the meaning an object once held for its producer and the ways that object was used, manipulated, and appreciated later in its life by another individual. While there is value in understanding the nature of the political or economic functions of objects at the time of manufacture, when we emphasize this aspect of an object's life over others we often strip away the connections between the object and its impact and import in the lives of colonial peoples. In ascribing the notion of "life" to an object, I wish to highlight the lives objects lead outside the context of the lifespan of an individual owner and how objects constrain and influence the lives of the people with whom they come in contact (Hill 2007; Miller 2005).

The eighteenth-century embroidered leather bag in Figure 1.4 provides an example of the changes in the life of an object as it moves from manufacturer to owner. The bag was most likely constructed by an Iroquois individual, and the porcupine and moose-hair embroidery that decorate the bag are similar to the decorations on other bags from the same period (Phillips 1998). What distinguishes this bag from others, however, is the use of a European military belt as its strap.

The iron belt buckle on the strap is likely French or English in origin. While the story of how the maker of this bag acquired the belt has been lost, one can imagine how these items might have changed hands in the context of French and Native American interactions during this period. The intention of the individual who sewed together these disparate pieces is also unknown. Was the action practical or was it an overt political statement?

1.4. Eighteenth-century smoked leather pouch embroidered with porcupine quills and moose hair. European military belt used as strap, probably Iroquois. Courtesy of President and Fellows of Harvard College, Peabody Museum of Archaeology and Ethnology, 67-10-10/301.

This hybrid object is just one example of the kinds of thoughtful manipulations of material objects that occurred in the colonial period.

If this bag had been recovered from an archaeological context, it would be unlikely that any leather would have remained, much less the detailed embroidery. In that case, would we have lost some of the intricate meanings that were invested in this composite object? Possibly. The interpretive potential this object poses inspires many of the discussions in this book. I wish to move beyond conservative interpretations to more fully explore that diversity of ways that objects of clothing and personal adornment were used to create, verify, and manipulate different identities throughout colonial America.

In the next chapter, I briefly outline artifacts of clothing and adornment found within the archaeological record. As other volumes identify and describe artifacts related to clothing (e.g., Deagan 2002; White 2005), here I describe just a few examples from the diverse range of objects of clothing and adornment available to people living in colonial North America. I do this not as a sourcebook for identification but rather as a way to understand methodological approaches used to interpret items of clothing and adornment within historical archaeology. I also include a discussion of practices that are rarely found in the archaeological record, such as tattooing, which must be considered when taking into account the adornment of the colonial body.

Following this I turn to case studies in North America and utilize archaeological, ethnographic, archival, and visual sources to investigate how people put together fashions through new and familiar forms of material culture to present the body and the self in colonial spaces. Each of the remaining chapters contains narrative- and object-centered vignettes that highlight meaningful intersections of the body, clothing, and adornment during the colonial period. The case studies discussed in these chapters include objects from the Peabody Museum's collection as well as items and collections from other published works and museum collections.

Chapter 3 provides a discussion of clothing artifacts related to the enclosures and alterations of the body, which include fasteners such as shirt buttons and lead seals attached to bales of cloth as well tattooed skin, another kind of enclosure. I follow this chapter with one that looks at adornment or objects that can be attached to the body or clothing, such as pierced coins, crucifixes, and glass beads. Chapter 5 provides a discussion of two assemblages of artifacts of clothing and adornment recovered from different parts of colonial North America. The ways that people used the objects of clothing and adornment in these assemblages in dressing practices were more varied and creative than those imagined by the manufacturers and suppliers of those items. The examples in this chapter consider the extent to which colonial individuals mixed different kinds of clothing and adornment in daily life.

I conclude the volume with a discussion of some current overarching themes and suggestions for future directions in the study of clothing and adornment in historical archaeology. Dress, clothing, and adornment played a central role in constructions of colonial American identities; and influenced dress in later centuries, including the Victorian period and beyond. The archaeological record provides insight into the ways that different peoples used clothing and adornment to make social statements, resulting in diversity of clothing and personal adornment found throughout colonial America.

2

~ ✣ ~

Discerning Artifacts
of Clothing and Adornment

There is new strength, repose of mind, and inspiration in fresh apparel.
—Ella Wheeler Wilcox

When one first considers the artifacts of dress, the universe of objects that could be defined as such seems quite contained: they are the objects a person chooses to cover or adorn his or her body. Buttons, buckles, belts, garments, and jewelry fit this definition, and most of these items are routinely recovered from colonial-period sites in North America. But the universe of what can be considered artifacts of clothing and adornment can be considerably greater than what we typically find in archaeological contexts; it can include leather, knit fabric, coins, guns, and knives. Furthermore, how an individual presented him or herself included other things that are not captured in the archaeological record very often, such as hairstyle, tattoos, impermanent body markings, posture, and language. For example, the Native Alaskan woman in Figure 2.1, a 1778 drawing by John Webber, the expedition artist for Captain John Cook's third voyage to the Pacific, is depicted wearing numerous items of adornment, tattoos, carefully dressed hair, and a finely made shirt (Figure 2.1). While these aspects of the dressed body rarely linger in the archaeological record of many areas of North America, all of these items were components of the way colonial selves were clothed and adorned.

Other excellent sourcebooks exist regarding how to identify and categorize items of clothing and adornment (see, for example, Deagan 2002; White 2005; White and Beaudry 2009). Rather than duplicate these fine efforts, I seek to track how colonial peoples from different contexts mobilized the same or similar items of clothing and adornment. I define artifacts of

2.1. *Woman of Oonalashka,* etching by John Webber, ca. 1778. Courtesy of President and Fellows of Harvard College, Peabody Museum of Archaeology and Ethnology, 41-72-10/504.

clothing as any items used to enclose or modify the physical body. These include fasteners for clothing, such as shoe buckles or buttons. I also include tattoos in this category, as the practice permanently marked or altered skin in ways that were often very visible. I also discuss items worn over clothing or adornments to the body such as necklace beads, crucifixes, guns, and pierced coins to be part of adornment strategies. In my examination of clothing and adornment in colonial North America, I draw from the archaeological, ethnographic, written, and pictorial records to capture the full range of what was and/or could be worn on an individual's body to provide a fuller consideration of ways that colonial peoples actively manipulated dress and adornment.

Categorizing Small Finds

Most items of clothing and adornment are categorized in archaeological practice as "small finds." Artifacts that fall into this category, such as buttons and buckles, are by definition small and often found in fewer numbers than other forms of material culture, such as glass and ceramics, as a result of depositional (they are often not found in archaeological excavation due to their size) and curatorial issues. Because of their scarcity, such artifacts tend to receive cursory attention in archaeological analysis and it is often presumed that as "personal" items their function is well-known; a button was used as a button (Beaudry 2006; Loren 2001b; Loren and Beaudry 2006; White 2005). For example, buttons and buckles are usually defined as items that attached clothing, while glass beads are often interpreted as trade goods. Likewise, religious medallions and crucifixes are considered to be symbols that indicate religious preferences, while guns and knives are lumped into the category of armament. As Beaudry (2006:7–8) notes, these categorizations limit our vision about how such objects were used in everyday life. This tendency is troublesome when one stops to consider the possible range of political and other ways people used items of dress.

Not surprisingly, the problem is historical, trapped within the logics of the practice of archaeology. The ever-growing body of literature that critiques the practices and biases inherent within the discipline of historical archaeology (and anthropology in general) (Beaudry 2006; Lightfoot 1995, 2004; Lightfoot et al. 1998; Loren 2001a, 2004, 2007a; Loren and Beaudry 2005; Silliman 2001, 2005; White 2005). For example, in 1935, when Charles C. Willoughby discussed the dress of the "Later Algonquian Group," in

Antiquities of the New England Indians, his analysis of objects of clothing and adornment focused on how Native peoples in the colonial period
adorned the dead. Willoughby's analysis was based on what types of material objects could be found in archaeological contexts in relation to narratives of dress in historical accounts.

> A . . . sheet copper band, twelve and one half inches in length, also with
> serrated edges, was taken from the grave of a child by Dr. Moorehead,
> at Sandy point, about five miles below Bucksport, on the Penobscot
> River. This grave contained also twenty-seven tubular beads of sheet
> copper and an iron axe. The beads were lying side by side on a piece
> of well-preserved buckskin which had been colored red and which
> was perfectly preserved, owing to contact with the copper. There were
> also a few white and blue discoidal beads of shell strung alternately on
> thong or sinew (Willoughby 1935:234–236).

Willoughby's discussion of this material was directly tied to Native American use of copper, a newly introduced metal in the sixteenth-century
northeastern United States. He discussed the buckskin and the beads that
accompanied the metal almost as an afterthought. These items were no
doubt an important aspect of this young individual's dressing practices and
that of his or her family. Yet any interpretation of what these materials
might have meant in the context of a child's burial is absent in the text, as is
any discussion of how these objects might have worked with each another
to constitute individual or group identity in death. That these interpretative aspects are missing from Willoughby's text is not surprising, given the
goals of his volume and his professional location as curator at Harvard University's Peabody Museum. Willoughby's primary concern was the artifact
as a specimen to be described, categorized, labeled, and stored within the
museum's collections.

Today, we often view such interpretations of artifacts as lacking the interpretive perspective that would speak to the intersection of self and object
in the construction of identity. But Willoughby's approach was pragmatic;
he was concerned with not only building an interpretative collection but
also with how objects could be managed within the walls of the museum.
Such management required the use of material-based categorization that
separated metal beads from glass beads, not only physically but also intel-
lectually. Even though our analysis has become more sophisticated since
Willoughby's time, the tendency to understand small finds by categorizing

them according to either function (based on assumptions about how an artifact was supposed to be used) or raw material lingers.

The set of categories most commonly used is the one developed by Stanley South in the 1970s as part of his effort to systematize how historical archaeologists approached artifact analysis (South 1977). South's clothing artifacts category included buttons and buckles, while his personal items category included glass beads, pipes, and so forth. He categorized guns and knives under "armaments." These categories have had such an influence on the discipline that it is difficult to find an archaeological catalog or site report that does not invoke South's ontological methods. There is certainly much utility to such a system when cataloging collections of artifacts recovered from specific field contexts. Yet such a system should be used as a guide to interpretation rather than as a system of categories that encompasses all the ways that individuals could use objects. We have much more to say about glass beads than simply that they were "personal items"; they were worn on the body, sewn onto clothing, used as rosary beads, woven into men and women's hair, and strung in necklaces. Despite critiques of this rigid scheme, many historical archaeologists continue to classify their finds according to South's categories. Put quite simply, it is useful for classification in museum and collections environments, but there is a need to move past any classificatory framework that hinders our exploration of the ways that many objects had multiple uses and multiple meanings for their users.

Critiques of museum practices and modern exhibits suggest that the process of storing and exhibiting objects is still hindered by colonial ideologies and needs to informed by current discourses on the ethics of stewardship (Colwell-Chanthaphonh and Ferguson 2007; Phillips 1998:68, 2005). Most would argue that while museum archives are rich repositories of information, they are also replete with stilted, problematic, or incorrect information. Some shortcomings stem from the ways that collectors cataloged their knowledge—the fieldwork methodology they use and the system they use to record and compile information that accompanies object inventories. Labels affixed to objects at the moment of excavation or accession may sometimes be misleading because they often represent the personal perspective or disciplinary bias of the excavator or collector. This is not to say that cataloging is incorrect (for how could museums function otherwise?) but rather that these acts force us to view collections in a certain way and that invariably the functions or meanings of objects are

2.2. Necklace with animal claws, glass beads, and thimbles, Ojibwa, Michigan. President and Fellows of Harvard College, Courtesy of Peabody Museum of Archaeology and Ethnology, 40-69-10/22746.

assigned by an individual who is not the person who used them. When using museum collections, and particularly when using isolated finds located within those collections, we must be aware of how museum practices of sorting collections by material type often lost or ignored information about the dynamic aspects of how objects in those collections were embodied by the people who used them. This is especially true of composite objects, such as the nineteenth-century Ojibwa necklace composed of animal claws, thimbles, goat and deer hooves, and green glass beads strung onto a narrow leather thong in Figure 2.2.

Using pattern analysis, the items that are part of this necklace would not fall into categories that would suggest sartorial or symbolic meanings. Rather, they would be relegated to categories that speak to their presumed function at the time of manufacture. Animal claws and goat and deer hooves would be analyzed as faunal remains, the brass thimbles could be used to interpret Ojibwa women's needlework, and the green glass beads would be no doubt interpreted in the context of trade with French and Anglo individuals living along the Great Lakes in the eighteenth and nineteenth centuries. Such categorization overlooks the diverse ways colonial peoples used material culture to meaningfully constitute their identities through dress. The same can be said of other categories of material culture that would seem to fall outside what one would consider to be a dress artifact, such as thimbles, coins, and even pieces of ceramic. Some of these items have been interpreted as trade items and analyzed in terms of political currency. But such interpretations strip away the personal aspects of these objects in daily use. Any study of dress must consider the social context instead of following ahistorical and decontextualized systems of categorization.

Three recent volumes offer contextual and textured interpretations of artifacts of clothing and adornment or artifacts of needlework related to clothing as aspects of identity making. Kathleen Deagan's second volume of *Artifacts of the Spanish Colonies of Florida and the Caribbean, 1500–1800* is devoted to small objects of personal possession, including items related to clothing and adornment (Deagan 2002). The outstanding contributions of Carolyn White (2005) and Mary Beaudry (2006) have brought further attention to the study of small finds. These three authors have guided and infused the growing historical archaeological discourse on clothing and adornment. Small finds related to clothing and adornment are everywhere, but because they are often found in small numbers the attention in historical archaeology has been focused on the larger finds of ceramics, pipes, and architecture, leaving items such as buttons and beads to languish in seemingly "meaningless categories" (Beaudry 2006:2).

This volume is meant to complement these fine works by examining objects of clothing and adornment from lesser-known colonial contexts and pausing to linger on examples that point to ways that people active manipulated items of clothing and adornment. This kind of research is necessarily interdisciplinary; it draws from historical documents and images and uses interpretive and methodological strategies from the disciplines of history and art history. My hope is to demonstrate how others might conceive of small finds in new and provocative ways.

Considerations Related to Texts and Visual Sources

Placing objects in historical context means more than being attentive to cataloguing, labeling, and provenance. It also means carefully critiquing the texts and images we use to draw out historical contexts. One of the great advantages of historical archaeology is the opportunity it provides to draw from a rich and diverse body of sources that includes material culture, texts, and historical images (Little 1992; Loren 2007b; Loren and Baram 2007; Mann 2007; Nassaney and Johnson 2000). Although the field of historical archaeology is often criticized for seeking direct correlates for material finds in historical or visual records (Beaudry 1988; Galloway 1991:457), when researchers use those sources carefully and analyze them critically, they can add valuable insights to the archaeological record. Historical accounts that include information about items of clothing, adornment, and the practices of dressing include diaries, account books, popular literature, newspaper accounts, wills, probate inventories, government reports, and diaries (see Beaudry 1988; Little 1992; White 2005:14–35).

Critically analyzing the historical record involves examining the author's background and training, the social context in which the text was written, the nature of the text, the method of observation the author used, whether the author used stereotypes, and the degree to which different observations corroborate with one another (Loren 2007a: 11–12; see also Galloway 1991; Lightfoot 1995, 2004; Stahl 1993; Wood 1990). Cultural stereotypes reflect cultural biases and perceptions about power relations between groups and are particularly evident in many colonial writings (Pagden 1982; Stahl 1993). In many cases, authors used cultural stereotypes that were partly or fully created long before the author had interacted with any of the people he or she was describing (De Moraes Farias 1985:30). Researchers must use these sources carefully to tease out reliable historical descriptions from stereotypes.

Images such as illustrations, watercolors, and maps seem to capture moments in time. While images provide a wealth of detail about the past, including visual information about specific forms and types of material culture that are useful in interpretations of the archaeological record, they also carry legacies of stereotypes and biases (Loren 2007a: 88; see also Beaudry 1988; King 2007; Loren 2007b; Loren and Baram 2007; Mann 2007). We need to consider the style, aesthetics, composition, and artistic themes that influenced the production and dissemination of colonial images (Loren 2007b; Mann 2007). For example, paintings such as *De Mulato y Mestisa Produce Mulato es Torna Atrás* (The Mulatto and Mestizo Produce a Mulatto Return-Backwards) illustrate the material aspects of differences in occupation, dress, comportment, and personal possessions (Figure 2.3). But one must keep in mind that the goal of such *casta* paintings produced in New Spain during the eighteenth century was to visually depict racial difference and racial hierarchies, including the many varieties of individuals

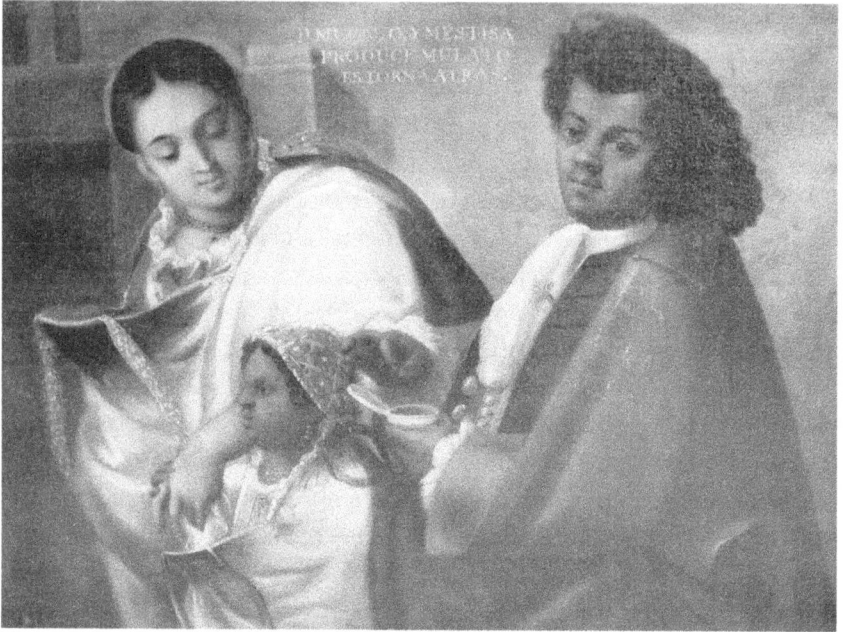

2.3. *De Mulato, y Mestisa Produce Mulato es Torna Atras* (From Mulatto and Mestizo, Mulatto Return Backwards), painting by Juan Rodríquez Juárez, ca. 1725. Courtesy of Sir Edward Hulse, Breamore House, Hampshire, England.

in the New World who were the offspring of parents of different racial groups (Carrera 2003; Katzew 2004; Voss 2008a:259–262).

Far from being a snapshot of colonial life, *casta* paintings reflect Spanish social classes and perceptions and racial hierarchies (Carrera 2003; Katzew 2004; see also Loren 2007a, 2007b; Pinney 1997; Voss 2008:259–262). Carrera (2003:6) describes how aspects of colonial identity—race, status, gender, wealth—were always subject to inspection. The body was a metaphor for colonial society; any weaknesses found in the body through the improper dress or actions of colonial subjects reflected the weaknesses of the ruling empire (Chaplin 2003; see also Hall 2000). Colonial paintings, illustrations, and writings were all about maintaining order. The *casta* paintings in New Spain were just one example of the tireless work of colonial officials and the Crown to fix specific visions of their empires. And much like colonial writings, these visual depictions were not completely accurate about the peoples and the contexts they sought to describe.

Given the biases inherent in these documents and images—which exist alongside the invaluable information such documents and images provide—how are we to make sense of this information in relation to the archaeological record? Martin Hall's work in historical archaeology (1992, 2000) offers important methodological avenues for working with texts, objects, and images. In his examination of colonial contexts in South Africa and the Chesapeake, he reminds us that government officials or elites often formulated textual and visual accounts in colonial centers. While these texts and images had weight with the proposed audiences, they represented a different reality than that of many who lived in the communities the officials were describing (Hall 1992; see also Baram 2007; Cannadine 2001; Loren 2007a; Loren and Baram 2007; King 2007; Pinney 1997; Mann 2007; Thomas 1991). In other words, such descriptions of colonial life often bore little relationship to reality. For example, sumptuary laws may have been accepted, disregarded, and/or redefined. Textual and visual accounts create discourses that inform us about the ideologically powerful perspectives of a few, not the views of the many. Critical examination of both ethnohistorical and visual records is crucial to uncovering biases within these records (Galloway 1991; Loren 2007a; Stahl 1993; Trouillot 1995; Wood 1990).

Sumptuary Laws and Their Impact on Fashion

Sumptuary laws enacted in the American colonies until the end of the eighteenth century are a particularly important source of information about colonial dressing practices. These were imperial mandates about how certain individuals were to clothe and adorn themselves with respect to gender, ethnicity, and status. Sumptuary laws also reinforced the fashion tastes of certain social groups. A glance back at Figure 1.1 indicates that Smibert, the artist who painted the portrait of the Berkeley group, took pains to depict his subjects dressed in the proper fashion, meaning that they were clothed in the textiles and styles that bespoke their position. A wealth of publications on the importance of colonial fashion indicates that what people wore and how they wore it were always concerns of those in power (e.g., Baumgarten 2002; Davis 1994; Hollander 1993; Lurie 2000).

Colonial dress in North America was characterized by combinations of locally made items and imported items. Both Native peoples and individuals of European and African descent made items of clothing and adornment. Mary Beaudry's recent work on artifacts of needlework and sewing illustrates how individuals living within the household were responsible for tailoring and mending (Beaudry 2006; see also Ulrich 2001). Making and mending clothing was a necessity: people needed clothing to stay warm. Yet clothing also embodied social and symbolic messages. Cultural standards determined what was considered "appropriate wear for a given person in a particular time and place" (Baumgarten 2002:54). These cultural standards shaped what Pierre Bourdieu (1984) refers to as "practices of taste," the everyday social habits that create a pattern that indicates class status and perpetuates social distinctions (Bourdieu 1984:2, 263). For example, during the seventeenth and eighteenth centuries, most women of European and African descent (who often were clothed by the former) wore long, full skirts and narrow bodices (Baumgarten 2002:60; see also Richardson and Kroeber 1952). The cut, construction, color, and fabric of a garment provided physical clues about the status and wealth of the woman wearing the skirt (Baumgarten 2002:64). Members of elite and non-elite groups were recognized in social arenas by their ability to maintain certain standards in clothing and adornment (Bourdieu 1984:7, 258; see also Mann and Loren 2001; Stahl 2001).

It is important to consider that in the colonial period, notions of taste and fashion were not only important for European elite, they were also important for the Native peoples, enslaved Africans, children, and working people who lived in colonial communities. The dress of European settlers was diverse: elite men in their frock coats, female servants in their homespun skirts, soldiers in uniform, and missionaries and priests in somber ecclesiastical garb each presented their bodies in ways that they deemed appropriate (Loren 2001b). Colonial authors were well aware that clothing and adornment was significant for many groups. For example, the French settler Antoine Le Page du Pratz, who was living in Louisiana in the first part of the eighteenth century, paired the trappings of fashion with notions of vanity, particularly for the young Natchez Indian men living in the colony:

> The youths are as vain as elsewhere, and are charmed to vie with one another in seeing who shall be the most dressed up, so much so that they put vermillion on themselves very often. They also put on bracelets made of the ribs of deer. . . . They wear necklaces like the women, and one sometimes sees them with a fan in the hand (Le Page du Pratz 1975:197–198).

Such narratives suggest that a mix of fashions could be found in colonial settings. Not only did people understand that clothing distinguished elites from non-elites, they also understood the differences in the fashions of individuals from other cultures, genders, and statuses. If we pair the image of Native and African peoples in Figure 1.2 with an image of French settlers, do we have a closer approximation of the fashions of people living in colonial New Orleans?

Possibly, but what measures were in place to ensure that people could be defined in the ways that they dressed? Certain types of fabric and items of adornment, such as wools, silks, and silver, were becoming increasingly available to those who lived outside the world of the nobility and the elite, and it was becoming increasingly difficult for colonial rulers to control how those items were used (Breen 2003; Ulrich 1991). Around the globe, many people who were not wealthy or influential wore the rich colors and sumptuous fabrics that had once marked the wearer as a member of the elite classes. For example, historian Timothy J. Shannon (1996) examines clothing exchanged between Mohawk and English settlers in eighteenth-century New York, noting how the exchange of fine clothing, such as ruffled shirts and frock coats, enabled some Mohawk leaders to transcend certain economic and diplomatic boundaries by strategically using of European-manufactured clothing. Colonial authorities in North America passed sumptuary laws because people commonly used clothing in ways that blurred the rigid social and political boundaries elites hoped to reinforce.

Sumptuary laws had a long history in the Old World. The first laws that regulated how people dressed, ate, and drank were established in ancient Rome as early as 187 B.C. (Hurlock 1984:65). Through the fifteenth through eighteenth centuries, sumptuary laws were commonplace throughout Europe, Asia, and the American colonies. For example, in France between 1485 and 1724, eighteen decrees were passed with regard to clothing and ornamentation to visually distinguish those who had titles from those who did not (Roche 1994:49, 100). Figure 2.4 depicts an etching by Abraham Bosse that was created in reaction to sumptuary laws; it portrays a courtier exchanging elaborate clothing for the sober dress demanded by the Edict of 1633.

The logic of sumptuary laws was simple: they were intended to restrict lavish dress in order to curb extravagance, protect fortunes, and visually mark the distinctions between levels of society. Clothing connoted status, gender, moral conduct, and education, and most individuals made clothing choices that were influenced by dress codes, social expectations,

LE COVRTISAN SVIVANT LE DERNIER EDIT   LE LACQVAY

2.4. *Le Courtesan suivant le Dernier Édit,* etching by Abraham Bosse, 1633. Public domain.

occupational necessities, status, and economics (Baumgarten 2002:42; Munns and Richards 1999:13). Sumptuary laws were an attempt by the nobility to safeguard what had been one of their privileges (the ability to dress well) from the advances of a rampant merchant class. They were intended to monitor the color, style, and fabric of what people wore. It was not just individual items that were important; the combinations of clothing and adornment a person wore and their comportment while wearing that garb were also crucial.

Because North American colonies were intended to be mirror images of their home communities (although few in practice actually achieved this goal), people living within those colonies were not free to choose their own fashion. For example, across the American colonies, enslaved Africans were generally prohibited from wearing any clothing that could be described as elegant (Mays 2004:231). Additionally, there were physical limits that constrained one's ability to negotiate self through fashion. For example, skin color and permanent skin markings may have left little room for negotiation or innovation of self through clothing and adornment.

In colonial New England, Puritans viewed flamboyant fashion as disorderly. The Massachusetts Bay Colony established sumptuary laws to enforce a modest and conservative style of dress among those living in the region. For example, Court of Boston decreed that low necklines and short sleeves were prohibited (De Marly 1990:35–38). In 1651, the Massachusetts legislature declared:

> our utter detestation and dislike, that men or women of mean condition, should take upon them the garb of Gentlemen, by wearing Gold or Silver Lace, or Buttons, or Points at their knees, or to walk in great Boots; or Women of the same rank to wear Silk or Tiffany hoods, or Scarfes, which tho allowable to persons of greater Estates, or more liberal education, is intolerable of people in low condition (quoted in Degler 1984:11).

Although these and other sumptuary laws enacted in the Massachusetts colony during the mid-seventeenth century were never truly enforced, they did imply that a difference in dressing style was to be maintained between lower and higher ranks and between those who were English and those who were not (De Marly 1990:37–38; Goodwin 1999:112). In the mid-Atlantic, Quakers were somewhat more relaxed about fashion than their Puritan persecutors, but men and women were prohibited from wearing clothes with gold and silver embroidery, hair ribbons, and powdered wigs (De Marly 1990:45). In Virginia and other southern English colonies, sumptuary laws were less strict, although certain stipulations about dress were still in place. For example, if an individual was worth less than £200 per year, he or she was expected to dress modestly (Mays 2004:384). Comments about dress were almost always coupled with attempts to regulate behavior. In seventeenth-century Virginia, the governor was instructed to "Suppress drunkedness gameing & excess in cloaths [and] not to permit any but ye Council & heads of hundreds to wear gold in their cloths" (quoted in Noël Hume and Noël Hume 2001:179).

Sumptuary laws in Dutch and French colonies were similar to those enacted in Europe (De Marly 1990:47–51). Titled women were to wear brightly colored (e.g., gold, red, purple) clothing, including skirts, petticoats, mantles, gowns, waistcoats, and bodices of fine fabrics (e.g., silk, damask, velvet) that were embroidered, fastened with gold and silver buttons, and worn with elaborate jewelry. Likewise, brightly colored waistcoats, breeches, doublets, hats, and coats distinguished titled men. Women of the

2.5. *De Español, y India, Produce Mestiso* (Spaniard and Indian Make Mestizo), Juan Rodríquez Juárez, ca. 1725. Courtesy of Sir Edward Hulse, Breamore House, Hampshire, England.

middling classes were prohibited from wearing certain colors (e.g., gold) and certain fabrics (e.g., silk). Instead, they were instructed to wear gray, black, and brown homespun linen and linsey-woolsey skirts, petticoats, and aprons. Instead of waistcoats and doublets, men of the middling classes were to wear plain breeches, hats, shoes, and coats (De Marly 1990:51–56; Loren 2001b).

Sumptuary laws in New Spain indicated that male Spanish settlers and soldiers in eastern Spanish Texas were to wear the Bourbon fashions of cutaway coats, embroidered vests, lace shirts, powdered wigs, and three-cornered hats, while Spanish women were to wear powdered wigs and dresses of silk or brocade adorned with ribbons or braid (Castelló Yturbide 1990:87). Only Spaniards were permitted to dress in silk, which was prohibited for all other groups (Klor de Alva 1996:65). Men and women of multiethnic ancestry as well as Africans were instructed to dress in the Bourbon fashion, mimicking fashions worn by elites using plainer styles and fabrics (Castelló Yturbide 1990:87). In the Spanish colonies, these laws were visually reinforced through the production of *casta* paintings such as the one in Figure 2.3 (Castelló Yturbide 1990; Loren 2007b; Voss 2008a). Over 500 *casta* paintings produced in New Spain during the eighteenth century distinguished individuals by race, by ethnicity, and by the dress that Spanish elites believed was appropriate to an individual's station in life (Figure 2.5).

Some colonial individuals were known for their predilection for mixing different dress styles. Fur trappers (*coureurs de bois*) in the French colonies and leatherstockings in present-day upstate New York wore a pastiche of different fashions that spoke to their identity as intermediaries between European and Native communities (Baumgarten 2002:65–66; Loren 2001a, 2001b; Shannon 1996). The practice of mixing different fashions was not unique to these frontier individuals. Even military figures from various colonies adopted some of the fashions of Native peoples. One example can be found in the writings of Fray Juan Agustín de Morfí, who described the dress of French, Spanish, and Native peoples living along the Louisiana-Texas border in the late 1700s:

> Most of the traders can scarcely be distinguished from the Indians. For they imitate them not only in their nakedness, but even in painting their faces. In testimony of this truth, I shall not quote any Spaniard but an illustrious and distinguished Frenchman. Such was Lieutenant-Captain Don Anthanase DeMézières called Captain Pinto, because he painted his face. . . . Referring to the woodsmen and Canadians scattered about Louisiana, and to the uniform which they should be obliged to wear . . . they should be obliged to wear them, because their greatest pleasure is to appear naked except for a breech-clout. Let us now see who abandon all decorum and go about unclothed. I surmise that only those of the lower class do this habitually, but it appears that some of the higher rank likewise do so (Hackett 1934:249).

Colonial authors, such as Morfí, sometimes argued that mixing different dress fashions was a necessity, that colonial peoples could not outfit themselves properly because of the European-manufactured clothing and cloth were not available in remote communities. But such configurations of dress were also purposeful; mixing fashions made for powerful political statements, to blur boundaries of difference, and allow for social movement.

Baumgarten (2002:74) points to the Native American dress worn by members of the Boston Tea Party as one example of the symbolic use of donning the fashions of another group.

In French and Spanish colonies, conversion was the goal of colonization, and colonial authors often praised Native Americans who dressed like them. For example, Father Charlevoix, a Jesuit who traveled through Louisiana between 1720 and 1722, commended a Tunica chief in 1720 for dressing like a European: "The chief received us very politely; he was dressed in the French fashion, and seemed to be not at all uneasy in that habit. . . . He has long left off the dress of a savage, and he takes pride [in] appearing always well-dressed, according to our fashion" (Swanton 1911:312–313). But in most American colonies, Native peoples were expected to dress according to their own fashions without the finery of elite European clothing. European colonists often reacted with disdain or mistrust when Native peoples donned European-manufactured clothing that was considered to be above their station. Additionally, many European colonists were concerned about the social and behavioral implications of unclothed flesh— that is, sin and barbarism (Loren 2001b, 2007a:96–97). Colonial officials anxious about "nakedness" would encourage Native peoples to cover their flesh by trading or selling certain objects of clothing or types of cloth to them. Silverman (2005:191) indicates that during the early eighteenth century, cloth, clothing, and sewing items made up a significant percentage of items that Wampanoag individuals purchased from Anglo merchants (see also Anderson 1994). Native peoples took advantage of the new materials and items that were thus available to them to produce new items of clothing to combine with other ready-made and locally produced clothing. Native American leaders were especially adept at this practice, particularly in diplomatic contexts, as seen in the engraving of Iroquois leader Joseph Fayadaneega (Brant) shown in Figure 2.6. This image illustrates how individuals combined clothing and adornment to embody certain political and social identities in specific cultural settings (Anderson 2005:84; De Marly 1990:102; Loren 2001b, 2007a).

Could one argue then that clothing and adornment practices are just a matter of fashion? Yes, in that fashion and style are often dictated or are often a direct response to social norms and conventions (see Hodder 1990). From seemingly unconscious choices to purposeful orchestration, dress was often manipulated to fit a particular social context. People choose strategies for clothing and adornment to embody notions of self that conformed

2.6. *Joseph Fayadaneega, Called the Brant, the Great Captain of the Six Nations*, mezzotint by John Raphael Smith, after a 1776 painting by George Romney. Courtesy of the Library of Congress.

to or emulated established fashions or subverted those fashions. But examples of mixed dress styles during the colonial period indicate that dress was not a straightforward matter of "putting on" a fashion. Instead, it was a process by which individuals created colonial identities at the intersection of taste, fashion, and sumptuary laws.

A Note on Context

Objects make their way into the archaeological record in a variety of ways. Many objects of clothing and adornment do so through everyday use and loss. Think of how many times a button is lost from a shirt. Such loss does not necessarily render a garment useless, however; another button can always be sewn in its place. The same holds true for glass beads that are lost from an embroidered shirt. Some items of clothing and adornment (perhaps especially adornment) may be passed down to family members because of the special meaning this item holds for the owner. Crucifixes and lockets are just a few items that come to mind. Yet these items also get lost or discarded to make their way into the archaeological record.

Perhaps the most common way that items of clothing and adornment are deposited in the archaeological record is when they were intentionally buried with an individual at the time of death. Many correlations have been made about an individual's (or even a larger group's) clothing and adornment practices in life based on what a person was wearing when they were buried (Meskell 2004; Nassaney 2004, 2005; Treherne 1995). In burials, it is not the single button, grommet, or glass bead that one usually finds in a household or midden context but often the whole item: the beaded shirt, trousers, rosary, or shoes. To see whole items of clothing and adornment associated with an individual body presents a picture that is compelling to the archaeologist: clearly this is how this individual dressed in his or her daily life. These were the combinations that were familiar to that individual and how he or she visually presented him or herself to the community at large.

But just as people manipulate clothing and adornment during their lives, these objects are manipulated by others at the time of burial. While some individuals dictate what they wish to wear when they are buried, more often the living choose such items for them to express certain beliefs about how a person should be dressed to meet his or her maker. Thus, the items of clothing and adornment we find with individuals may represent the beliefs and tastes of the individual being buried or they may represent the beliefs and values of those who are burying the individual. Mortuary practices can mark, mask, or naturalize social relations (Hodder 1990). The tendency to view the body in death as a direct analog of the body in life is strong, particularly when looking at items of clothing and adornment that were recovered near an individual. My point here is that the items of clothing and adornment found with an individual in death represent only a portion of their expressions of clothing and adornment in life. These items provide only a narrow view of an individual's wardrobe, their sartorial repertoire for constituting self through clothing and adornment. Likewise, while I include ethnographic material in many of the examples discussed in this volume, I always keep in mind that ethnographic materials have been filtered through the eye and taste of the collector and that collections often speak more to the collector's and curator's preoccupations than they do to those of the person(s) who created and used them.

Any discussion of the body in death in the context of North America must include some discussion of the Native American Graves Protection and Repatriation Act (NAGPRA). Passed in 1990, this federal legislation (43 CFR 10) mandates that Native American human remains and associated funerary objects be repatriated to federally recognized indigenous groups for which a relationship of "shared group identity" can be determined. Moral and ethical debates about the politics of NAGPRA and continuing relationships and collaborations between anthropologists and Native peoples redound in contemporary literature, which focuses largely on the processes of consultation between institutions and tribal representatives and on the physical return of remains (see, for example, Capone and Loren 2004; Scarre and Scarre 2006; Vitelli and Colwell-Chanthaphonh 2006; Watkins 2005; Zimmerman et al. 2003).

In museums, cultural material from colonial America that is subject to NAGPRA often constitutes a sizable portion of collections. Such material now falls into the categories of culturally affiliated (cases where a relationship of shared group identity has been established) or culturally unidentifiable (cases where such a relationship cannot be made). In the time since the passing of NAGPRA, many culturally affiliated human remains and cultural items have been published in the Federal Register, have been physically repatriated, or have been reburied, while others are awaiting their return home and remain under the care of the museum (Capone and Loren 2004).

Several of the examples used in this volume are derived from funerary contexts, some of which have been published in the Federal Register as funerary objects. While many items have returned to their communities and others are in the process of making their way home, collections subject to NAGPRA contain important information about colonial life. Multiple stakeholders have an interest in any collection (whether it is subject to NAGPRA or not) and we must be aware of our responsibilities regarding the interpretation of this material for the public and for descendant communities. Archaeological approaches to these collections are not necessarily more valid than the interpretations of descendant communities, but it should be the case that all parties are concerned with issues of preservation, dignity, conservation, and community access. Such topics are particularly important within museums, now arenas of negotiation and resolution, where the primary goal is to interpret the past for the public while simultaneously acting as responsible stewards of collections of great importance to descendant communities.

3

~ ✿ ~

Enclosing the Body

She wears her clothes as if they were thrown on with a pitchfork.
—Jonathan Swift

Very few examples of complete clothing survive in the archaeological record of much of colonial America. What usually remain are parts of complete articles of clothing: clothing fasteners such as buttons from a shirt
or coat and metal buckles from leather and fabric shoes. Shreds of woven
and knit fabric have also been recovered, but much more common are
the lead seals that were attached to bolts of European-produced cloth that
were shipped into the colonies. Whole pieces of fully fashioned clothing
were also regularly imported into colonial America (hats, dresses, shirts).
Sewing and tailoring were common activities in the American colonies,
where professional male tailors were charged with clothing the local population (Baumgarten 2002:52). For example, seven tailors were living in the
community of Jamestown in the English colony of Virginia in 1608 (Kelso
and Straube 2000:46). In the household, seamstresses were responsible
for clothing the occupants and mending their clothes (Beaudry 2006). At
Andrew Jackson's plantation, for example, clothing and shoes for the enslaved Africans living there were made on site by women in a style that
was created and approved by the overseers (Galle 2005:41). Archaeological evidence of sewing activities includes needles, straight pins, thimbles,
bodkins, and awls (Beaudry 2006). With the exception of Mary Beaudry's
Findings: The Material Culture of Needlework and Sewing (2006), little has
been written from an archaeological perspective about the tools used in
sewing and needlework (see Ulrich 2001).

This pattern of combining handmade articles with imported ones gener-
ated some amount of critique. Even colonists were scandalized by the ways

their neighbors mixed fashions. In a 1619 letter, John Pory, secretary of the Virginia Company at Jamestown, complained about this issue in letters to the Company:

> Noew that your lordship may knowe, we are not the veriest of beggers in the worlde, our Cowe-keeper here of Iames city on Sundayes goes acowtered in freshe flaming silkes and a wife of that in England had professed the black arte not of a scholler but of a collier of Croydon, weares her rough beauer hat with a faire perle hatband, and a silken suite (quoted in Bach 2000: 10).

As Bach (2000:11) explains, this quote is just as much about the disdain for inferiors as it is about disdain for the sartorial freedom in the New World: a keeper of cows felt that he had the right to wear scarlet silk clothing, a privilege usually restricted to noblemen, while the wife of a common laborer decorated her beaver hat with a bejeweled hatband and wore silk. This example is just one among many of sumptuary laws being ignored while peoples forged their own fashion in colonial America.

In this chapter, I examine how colonial peoples covered their skin and track how different peoples in colonial America used common imported items. I am especially interested in how colonial individuals used material culture in new and unique combinations to counter social mores and expectations. There are far too many examples of artifacts that relate to covering skin than can be covered in this brief chapter—such as shoes, hats, shirts, and doublets—so here I track three examples. The first is a practice rarely (if ever) captured in the archaeological record, but it is the most intimate method of covering one's skin: tattooing and scarification. While such bodily enclosures rarely leave an archaeological signature, these practices were an important aspect of colonial life and were extraordinary statements of personal identity. Native and non-Native peoples practiced different ways of permanently altering their skin through tattooing and other forms of permanent markings as one layer of self-presentation. In the second example, I discuss the kinds of cloth that moved through colonial communities and to suggest some of the ways this cloth was used to clothe the body. In the final section of the chapter, I follow one kind of clothing fastener—in this instance a common eighteenth-century shirt button—across different parts of the Atlantic world.

Marking the Body: Tattoos and Other Skin Modifications

Archaeological perspectives on colonial clothing and adornment rarely take into account changes made to the body proper through permanent modifications. Tattooing, branding, and self-flagellation left little evidence in the archaeological record, but tools to mark the skin (tattoo needles) and other practices of altering skin by cosmetics, prosthesis (let us not forget George Washington's wooden teeth), hairstyles and piercings do leave a small archaeological signature. Moreover, historical documents indicate how common and visually important such markings were in social presentations of the colonial body. Using this evidence, social anthropologists have sought to interpret colonial bodily modifications (e.g., Caplan 2000; Chaplin 1997; Lindman and Tarter 2001; Thomas et al. 2005). My intention in including a section on tattooing and body modification is to underscore the importance of bodily modification in the colonial world. An individual's body, including skin color, gender, and markings, was the canvas on which he or she placed items of clothing and adornment, and individuals often manipulated this canvas to signal political messages.

Colonial identity was as much physical as it was material (Chaplin 1997:229). During the colonial period, the color and quality of an individual's skin featured prominently in imperial hierarchies and heavily scrutinized; it marked where you fit within the colonial world. Colonial discourse about the body was fundamental to most imperial projects, especially during the eighteenth century when racial ideologies were beginning to be promulgated in the New and Old Worlds (Chaplin 1997:233; see also Chaplin 2003; Orser 2007; Pagden 1982). Colonial officials and authors were particularly interested in using skin color as a visual marker between colonized and colonizer, elite and non-elite. Concerns about skin color were closely linked to expectations about how individuals should dress, as can be seen in the *casta* painting depicted in Figure 2.5. People could then be classified not only by the color of their skin but also by how they dressed (if they covered their bodies at all), what they ate, and what they did for a living (Loren 2001b).

Tattoos were common among Native American groups throughout colonial America. These practices were an integral aspect of body presentation because they symbolized rank, knowledge, gender, and power (Jackson 1994). Both men and women were tattooed in highly visible places such as the face, arms, and legs. Most of these tattoos were black and red,

3.1. *Saturiova Re della Florida nell America Setentrional in atto di andare alla Guare*, drawing by Jacques LeMoyne de Morgues, ca. 1588. Courtesy of President and Fellows of Harvard College, Peabody Museum of Archaeology and Ethnology, 41-72-10/446.

but colonial authors also described blue and green tattoos (Volo and Volo 2002:24). Bodily markings were of such interest to the European public that many historical images and descriptions of this practice exist. For example, Jacques Le Moyne de Morgues, a Huguenot artist and member of Jean Ribault and René Goulaine de Laudonnière's French expedition to the eastern coast of present-day Florida in 1564, depicted them on La Florida's inhabitants in a series of drawings (Le Moyne 1875:2; Moser 1998:72).

Le Moyne's illustrations (which were later copied by Flemish engraver Theodor de Bry) provide intricate detail about the sixteenth-century lives of Native Floridians. Like other travel narratives of its time, this ethnographic documentation was tied to the curiosity of Europeans about otherworldly exoticism. It documented many types of behavior and customs, including clothing, adornment, diet, and tattooing. Many Native American groups understood tattooing as a kind of clothing because it covered the skin while simultaneously presenting personal information about lineage, status, and identity (Sayre 1997:166; see also Loren 2001b). The Timucuan man depicted in Figure 3.1 wears shell earspools, a feathered headdress, a piece of fabric around his privates, and a pelt. Tattoos cover the rest of his body, and the density of tattooing covers his exposed skin so fully that to our modern eye he appears to be covered as if clothed in fabric.

European authors tried to understand the meaning behind Native American practices of tattooing skin and descriptions of marks and meanings were often included in historical accounts. For example, Thomas Hariot's *A Briefe and True Report of the New Found Land of Virginia*, which included Theodor de Bry's engravings of John White's drawings, provided an interpretation of tattoos so that Europeans who would likely never travel to North America could understand them. Plate 23 of this book features images of tattooed Algonquian people from the mid-Atlantic (Figure 3.2).

The caption that accompanies this image reads:

> The Marckes of sundrye of the Cheif mene of Virginia. The inhabitāts of all the cuntrie for the most parte haue marks rased on their backs, wherby yt may be knowen what Princes subiects they bee, or of what place they haue their originall. For which cause we haue set downe those marks in this figure, and haue annexed the names of the places, that they might more easelye be discerned. Which industrie hath god indued them withal although they be verye sinple, and rude.

And to confesse a truthe I cannot remember, that euer I saw a better or quietter people then they.

The marks which I obserued a monge them, are heere put downe in order folowinge.

The marke which is expressed by A. belongeth tho Wingino, the cheefe lorde of Roanoac.

That which hath B. is the marke of Wingino his sisters husbande.

Those which be noted with the letters, of C. and D. belonge vnto diverse chefe lordes in Secotam.

Those which haue the letters E. F. G. are certaine cheefe men of Pomeiooc, and Aquascogoc. (Hariot 1590:Plate 23).

Although Europeans were familiar with tattooing, their preference for white, unblemished skin (usually obtained through cosmetics) led them to view tattooed skin and the person housed within that skin with fascination, disdain, and suspicion (Morgan and Rushton 2005). During the seventeenth and eighteenth centuries, European explorers and missionaries encountered tattooed peoples throughout North America and Oceania

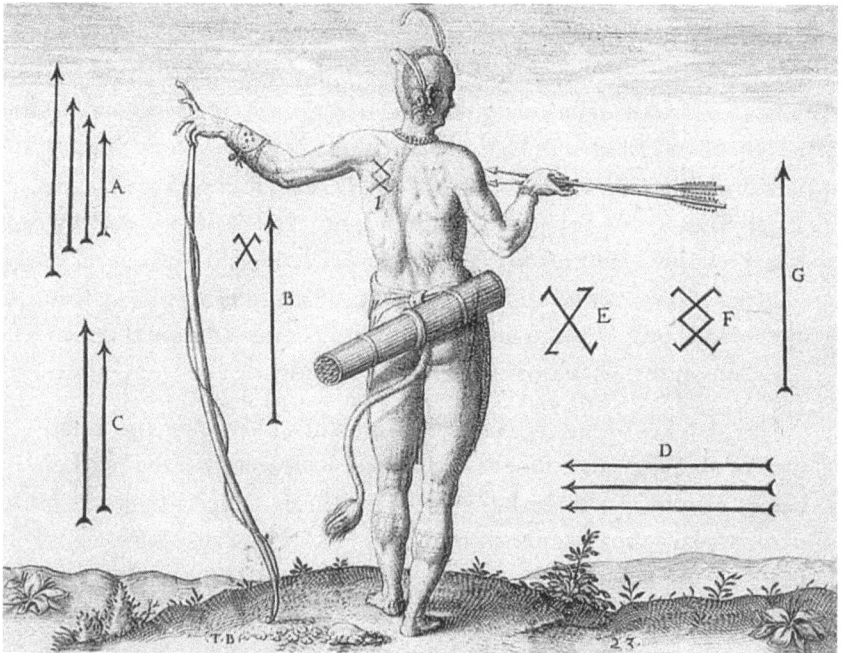

3.2. "The Marckes of sundrye of the Cheif mene of Virginia." Plate 23 in Thomas A. Hariot, *A brief and true report of the new found land of Virginia,* 1590.

(Thomas et al. 2005). This body art was a powerful stimulus for Europeans, and sailors often returned from their voyages sporting elaborate tattoos. However, these markings soon became associated with the criminal classes. Morgan and Rushton's (2005) analysis of late eighteenth- and nineteenth-century court records illustrates how the bodies of convicts as well as those of the poor were often marked with tattoos. For example, a 1739 English newspaper described a convicted thief as:

> a Rogue of about 15 years of age convicted of stealing Weights out of Sadler's Shop in the Borough, from a Natural Propensity to Villainy, had on his Breast, mark'd with Indian ink, the Poutraiture of a Man at length, with a Sword drawn in one Hand and a Pistol discharging Balls from the Muzzle in the other, with a Label from the Man's Mouth, G-d d-amn you, stand. This the Rogue would have conceal'd, but a Discovery being made thereof, he was order'd to shew his Breast to the Court, who were all shock'd at so uncommon a Sight in so young a Ruffian. (*Newcastle Courant,* January 27, 1739, quoted in Morgan and Rushton 2005:51)

By the eighteenth century, European soldiers and sailors were being tattooed with more frequency. This behavior was seen as scandalous in most heavily Catholic European countries. For example, in eighteenth-century France, Christian men simply did not tattoo their skin. Yet after their first interactions with Native peoples of the Southeast, French soldiers (who were in America for their king and their God) often tattooed their bodies, to the horror of the Jesuit priests who accompanied them on their travels. Henri de Tonti's 1697 account describes a soldier of "breeding" as being permanently marked with Christian symbols (Mary, Jesus, and a crucifix) as well Native American symbols and a depiction of a snake pointing toward his genitals (Sayre 1997:170–171). Not only was dress implicated in this account but also manner and comportment. Reports such as this led government and religious leaders to complain about the breakdown of French civilization. Yet this account also suggests that it was not only lower-status French subjects who were acting improperly; the soldier de Tonti described was a man of breeding, an elite who had been seduced into going native.

As Europeans encountered tattooed individuals more often and learned more about the practice, more of them wanted to be tattooed, suggesting that there was something inherent in the American experience that shifted the consciousness of some individuals about tattooing and unblemished skin. Sayre (1997:178–179) describes how French soldiers and colonial officials began to understand how Native American tattooing marked the status and bravery of individuals as warriors. For Europeans in the New World who chose to have themselves tattooed in the "Native manner," these markings, while permanent, were only temporary tokens of "power and prestige" because Europeans who stayed in the Old World would never understand them in the same way. In other words, the symbolism of the markings worked only in the New World context (Sayre 1997:179).

Some markings made on the skin were far from voluntary, as is illustrated by the eighteenth-century practice of branding the skin of African slaves. Morgan and Ruston (2005:47) provide an example from an eighteenth-century newspaper account from Philadelphia:

> Advertised in Philadelphia was one mulatto slave called Dave, owned by Henry Miller, "branded on the forehead with the letter M." This may have been a brand inflicted by the master himself, probably after an escape attempt. In 1766, Virginian Robert Munford advertised that a "fellow named Jack," involved in "promoting the late disorderly meetings among the Negroes," had run off for fear of being prosecuted for many felonies. He had red eyes, and had been branded with "R" on one cheek, and "M" on the other.

In the context of slavery, branding was perhaps the most aggressive act of body marking, especially when it was done to the face, the place on the body most available for public view (Burton 2001:57). While branding may have been voluntary in other world cultures during the eighteenth century (an example would be the penitential self-flagellation of Jesuits), in colonial America the act of branding enslaved peoples connoted complete power and ownership over another person's body and control of all of that person's bodily acts. This kind of body marking would permanently state to the public at large—for an individual's whole life—that the branded person was owned by another human being.

Few implements used in tattooing and branding are found in the archaeological record of colonial America; most museum examples date to the nineteenth century. Tattoo needles have been recovered from colonial sites in Hawaii and some archaeologists have speculated that metal and bone awls found at historical sites may have been used not only for cutting through leather but also for marking the skin (Kirch 1997:197; Parker Pearson 1999:84). A recent archaeological find of a cilice from Fort St. Joseph, an eighteenth-century French, Miami, and Potawatomi community located in present-day Niles, Michigan, provides new insight into colonial practices of self-mortification (Brandão and Nassaney 2008; Nassaney 2008). Devout Catholics use cilices to punish the flesh (Brandão and Nassaney 2008). The cilice recovered from the site of Fort St. Joseph was a metal instrument worn underneath clothing that would pierce the flesh of a person's arm or leg as he or she moved about. The Catholics of New France would have used such an item to atone for their sins and to control sexual desire, a constant concern in the New World, where many French settlers were tempted by the flesh of Native peoples (Brandão and Nassaney 2008; see also Loren 2001b).

Covering the Body: Lead Cloth Seals

A sense of the variety of cloth commonly brought to the American colonies can be found in a 1761 account of goods shipped to Charlestown. The shipment included:

> Duggets, drabs, duffles, duroys, serges, and shalloons, camlets, and grosgrams, cloth broad and narrow, from fine broadcloth to Negro cloth, Cloathes ready made for an enormous importation, also blankets, flannels, hats in wool or beaver, stockings, shrouds, carpets, buttons and mohair. Linen from Cambrick to Onnabrig, sail cloth linen, ticking, chequered and printed Linens, haberdashery items, East Indian cottons, calico, white or printed, muslin, dimity and fustian. English silks, stockings, Indian's silks, handkerchiefs, gloves, ribbons, and Laces (quoted in De Marly 1990:88).

Cloth was one of the most important items exported from Europe to the colonies during the seventeenth and eighteenth centuries (Breen 1993; Ulrich 1991; see also Anderson 1994; Welters et al. 1985). Thousands upon thousands of yards of imported textiles were shipped to the American colonies each year. Plain linens imported from Ireland, Scotland, and northern England were used for men's shirts, women's shifts, and summer outerwear for slaves and laborers (Baumgarten 2002:78). Wool textiles produced in England, including broadcloth and damask, were used for trousers, cloaks and overcoats (Baumgarten 2002:78). Cotton and cotton-linen blends that were obtained from Lancashire, England, were used for shirts, shifts, and chemises (Baumgarten 2002:79). English weavers also supplied most of the silks that were used for doublets, dresses, and other finery (Baumgarten 2002:83). In Amsterdam, Kampen weavers specialized in making a woolen fabric known as "duffel," a coarse fabric commonly used for blankets, cheap coats, and shoe insoles (Baart 1987:8). Red stroud, a heavy woolen fabric produced in the Gloucestershire town of Stroud, was often imported for trade primarily with Native Americans, but European and African peoples used it as well (Adams 1989:14).

English wool and French *écarlatine* (scarlet cloth) were also popular among Native American consumers (Adams 1989:14). Welters and colleagues (1985) record the broad range of European fabrics recovered from two seventeenth-century mortuary contexts: a Narragansett cemetery in Rhode Island (RI-1000) and a Mashantucket Pequot cemetery in eastern Connecticut (Long Pond). Textiles recovered from these sites include wool, linen, and silk as well as Native American-manufactured textiles. Their documentation of a variety of types of European-manufactured cloth in Native American contexts indicates that trade in cloth and European-manufactured clothing had expanded in North America by the middle of the seventeenth century.

European-manufactured cloth was traded with Native American consumers for a variety of reasons, secular and sacred (see Loren 2001b). Cloth was a physical medium for the religious reform of Native peoples: it would cover their nakedness and thus enable them to be recognized as Christian and civilized. For example, in a 1609 broadside entitled "Nova Britannia," Robert Johnson discussed the need for imported cloth to trade with Algonquian peoples living in present-day Virginia:

> But of all things, that God hath denied that countrie, there is want of Sheepe to make woolen cloth, and this want of cloth must alwais bee supplied from England, whereby when the colony is thorowly increased, and the Indians brought to our ciuilitie (as they will in short time) it will cause a mighty vent of English clothes.

Although documentary sources provide ample information about the kinds of cloth that were being shipped into the American colonies for Native and non-Native peoples, remnants of colonial cloth in archaeological contexts are rare. When recovered, these small scraps provide detailed information about how cloth was used to fashion clothing within colonial communities. For example, Ordoñez and Welters (1998) analyzed over 150 fragments of cloth recovered from a seventeenth-century privy located behind the Nanny House site on Cross Street in Boston, Massachusetts. The types of fabric in the assemblage included a wide variety of silk, wool, and cotton (Ordoñez and Welters 1998). Scissors, a needle case, a large number of silk ribbons, scraps with cut edges, and fabrics that show different seaming and construction techniques suggest that Katherine Nanny-Naylor, the resident of the house, sewed, mended, and embellished her family's clothing.

Archaeological contexts are often not conducive to the preservation of textiles such as those recovered from the Katherine Nanny-Naylor privy. However, lead seals originally attached to bolts of cloth, which are often recovered in archaeological contexts, provide evidence of the distribution and types of textiles that were used in colonial contexts.[1] These seals were typically two lead discs joined by a connecting strip that were folded around each side of a textile and stamped closed. Lead seals were attached to the outside corner section of bolts of cloth as a means of identification and as a component of regulation and quality control. The marks on the seals provide information about place of manufacture, taxation, or local inspection by dyers, clothiers, or weavers (Luckenbach and Cox 2003). Most textiles exported in this period were produced by guilds of weavers rather than in factories (Adams 1989:16). Every textile produced in Europe during this period was subject to inspection to ensure the quality of the threads used, the warp and weft, and the selvedge and the consistency of dye (Reddy 1988:266). Additionally, archaeologically recovered lead seals sometimes maintain the impression of the textile to which they were stamped. By the nineteenth century, lead seals had become obsolete due to industrialized production of textiles (Adams 1989:18).

Although lead seals were small items that were easily lost from bolts of cloth, they have been recovered from colonial sites throughout North America, including in domestic contexts. The locations of the cloth seals that have been recovered suggest how cloth was used within the household and in other community settings. For example, several lead cloth seals recovered from the cellar of Harvard's Old College building in Cambridge, Massachusetts, suggest that the people living there constructed their own clothing. In the late 1980s, excavations conducted in the center of present-day Harvard Yard revealed the cellar of one of the university's first four buildings, the Old College, which was built in 1644 (Stubbs 1992). By 1678, the wooden building was falling in on itself, and it was eventually torn down. Archaeological investigations of Old College indicated that the cellar

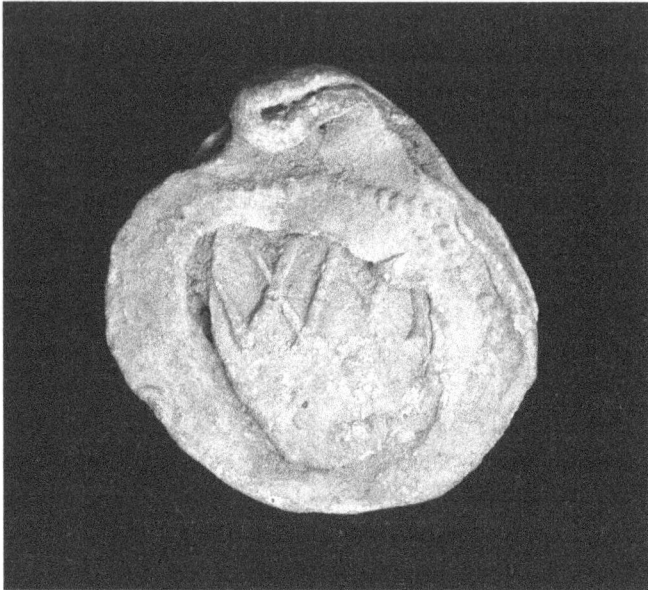

3.3. English lead cloth seal from Old College Cellar, Harvard Yard, Cambridge, Massachusetts. Courtesy of President and Fellows of Harvard College, Peabody Museum of Archaeology and Ethnology, 987-22-10/100195.

was filled through several refuse deposits from the late seventeenth through the early eighteenth centuries. The seal depicted in Figure 3.3 is embossed with the initial "W" (or "WM") and was likely attached to woolen fabric, perhaps from the London Dyers' Company (Egan 1995).

That this site offers evidence suggesting that the inhabitants of the site wore English-made clothing is not surprising. This particular New England context was a bastion of Puritan ideology, where English and Native American students were trained in "knowledge: and godlines[s]" (Harvard Charter of 1650, Harvard University Archives). Students of the university followed the sumptuary laws dictated by the Massachusetts Bay Colony, and the university forbade the wearing of "rich and showy clothing" (Harvard College Laws 1700, Harvard University Archives). Worsted wool would have fit within what Harvard and the Massachusetts Bay Colony considered "proper" clothing; this fabric was used to construct or mend plain trousers, overcoats, or scholars' gowns. Another example of what Puritans considered to be proper fashion comes from the writings of Increase Mather, later president of Harvard, who in 1679 noted:

A proud Fashion no sooner comes to this Country, but *haughty Daughters of Zion* in this place are taking it up, and thereby the whole land is at last infected. What shall we say when men are seen in the Streets with monstrous and horrid *Perriwigs*, and Women with their *Borders and False Locks* and such like whorish Fashion, whereby the anger of the Lord in kindled against this sinful Land! (quoted in Goodwin 1999:111–112, emphasis in original text).

Most lead seals I have researched originate from the European empire. For example, almost 40 lead cloth seals were recovered from seventeenth-century sites in Anne Arundel, Maryland, as part of the Lost Towns Project (Luckenbach and Cox 2003). The seals recovered were English in origin, indicating that this community obtained cloth exclusively from Britain, such as Kersey woolen twill commonly used for overcoats (Luckenbach and Cox 2003).

European-manufactured cloth was brought to Colonial America for a variety of consumers: not just European colonists but also Native peoples, enslaved Africans, and servants. The recovery of hundreds of cloth seals from Fort Michilimackinac, an eighteenth-century fur-trading village and military outpost located in present-day Mackinaw City, Michigan, provides detailed information about the exchange between fur traders and cloth importers and the intersection of the trade of these two categories of material. The fort was a major hub of the growing fur trade in the Great Lakes region during the second half of the eighteenth century (Adams 1989:1; Morand 1994). As Adams (1989:1) explains, goods such as cloth, Jesuit rings, and clothing were brought to the fort from Montreal to be sent to other traders in the region or traded with the Odawa (Ottawa) peoples living nearby for fur. The rhythm of the fur trade and of colonial exchanges in this region generally followed the pattern found in other regions: Native American trappers and traders trapped and processed furs that they exchanged for European-manufactured items (Sokolow 2003:150). European-manufactured cloth was in high demand among Native American consumers. Dean Anderson's examination of Montreal merchant records indicates that wool produced in France and England as well as thread, yarn, leggings, chemises, linen and cotton shirts, wool doublets, waistcoats, and sleeves constituted the vast majority of goods sent to Fort Michilimackinac (Anderson 1991, 1994; see also Anderson 1991, 1994; Kent 2001:546–562).

Extensive excavations of Fort Michilimackinac revealed more than 250 lead seals from French and British occupations of the site (Adams 1989:1). The embossed markings and cloth imprints on most of these seals indicate that they were originally attached to French or English cloth. Included in the assemblage are 16 seals from French *écarlatine* produced in Mazanet, 13 seals from French *bays* (a type of wool), one seal from common English grey wool, 20 seals from French woolen stockings, and two seals from Lyons silk (Adams 1989:38–43). These lead fabric seals provide evidence of just a portion of the kinds of cloth shipped to the fort that was then used to make clothing.

As with many other colonial sites, the lead fabric seals recovered from the fort indicate that its population constructed clothing from imported cloth that was appropriate to the community of soldiers that lived there (leggings and wool intended for trousers, for example), some silk for fine clothes (intended for elites), and large quantities of bright scarlet cloth intended for trade with neighboring Odawa communities (Anderson 1991; see also Kent 2001:540–546). As members of *Compagnies franches de la marine*, soldiers at Fort Michilimackinac wore a uniform that consisted of a long collarless single-breasted grayish-white coat (*justaucorps*), a blue long-sleeved waistcoat, breeches, and stockings (Volo and Volo 2002:186). Dress for civilian men usually included trousers, shirts, cloaks, and coats, while women often wore, shirts, petticoats, aprons, chemises, bodices, and pockets (Kent 2001:581).

When the evidence we find meets our expectations about dress and its related artifacts, does it indicate that people wore the dress that was expected of them? In the case of Fort Michilimackinac, lead fabric seals alone do little to adjust our preconceived vision of daily life. The lead fabric seals recovered from Fort Michilimackinac were removed from bales, and the cloth in those bales was cut into smaller lengths for trade. But what evidence exists that the lead seals from scarlet cloth that were found throughout the site were removed not just so the cloth could be cut for trade but also so it could be cut to construct clothing? We assume that the scarlet cloth was cut for trade because of published contemporary reports that state that red woolen cloth was used for trade with Native peoples. A more careful reading of historical accounts, however, can provide more information about how settlers at the site dressed. Through these documents, a different version of clothing at the fort emerges. Numerous settler accounts stated that they were desperate for clothing and sought the help of Odawa women as well as tailors who lived on the site (Morand 1994:68). Items associated with sewing and tailoring—needles, thimbles, and scissors—have been recovered from numerous context at Fort Michili-mackinac (Morand 1994:69). Settlers combined locally made and imported clothing at Fort Michilimackinac; narratives from visiting dignitaries and colonial leaders indicate that settlers and soldiers (not just *coureurs du bois*) often wore moccasins, breechclouts and leggings in combination with ruffled shirts and waistcoats adorned with gilt braid (Morand 1994:67–68; Kent 2001:555).

Although company warehouses were stocked with numerous fabrics and articles of clothing, such as coats, cloaks, and trousers, these items were not always accessible to everyone at the fort (Anderson 1991, 1994; Kent 2001:569). Moreover, the clothing in the warehouses may not have been appropriate to how people at the fort lived their lives; they may have chosen to combine leggings and ornate waistcoats for more practical reasons. These combinations of dress are telling regarding how soldiers and settlers chose to dress in a fur trade town: they opted for a combination of imported and locally made goods to create a style of dress that was relevant in their part of the colonial world.

Fastening Cloth to Skin: Common Shirt Buttons

Historical archaeologists have long been preoccupied with buttons found at historical sites. As White (2005: 50) states, "Buttons are the most common type of personal adornment artifact recovered on historical-period archaeological sites; they are found in great numbers and in multitudinous designs, materials, forms, and sizes." Cheryl Claassen (1994) has provided detailed information about shell button production, an important aspect of American manufacturing in the nineteenth and twentieth centuries. And White (2005) provides great detail about the production, distribution, and recovery of buttons in seventeenth- and eighteenth-century New England. This research on buttons complements other work on buttons in many publications in historical archaeology (e.g., Aultman and Grillo 2003; Hinks 1988; Noël Hume 1969; White 2005). Because buttons have been so extensively examined within the discipline, the question is not whether or not to include them as a category; the question is whether more can be said about this mundane object.

3.4. One-part stone button mold, Lincoln, Massachusetts, seventeenth century. Courtesy of President and Fellows of Harvard College, Peabody Museum of Archaeology and Ethnology, 24-7-10/94279.

As White (2005:73) and others have noted, there is still much to say. Buttons are used to simultaneously enclose the body and adorn the body. During the sixteenth and seventeenth centuries, only military men and wealthy colonists normally used buttons. Everybody else fastened their simple clothing with laces tipped by metal ends known as aglets. During the seventeenth and eighteenth centuries, plain and ornate buttons adorned coats, underwear, vests, and shirts. The style, shape, size and manufacture of a button can indicate what kind of clothing was worn. For example, brass buttons are from military coats, while we know that fabric-covered buttons were used on long underwear.

Prior to the eighteenth century, only a small amount of button production occurred in North America. Rather, as White indicates (2005:50–52), until the second half of the eighteenth century, most button production occurred in Europe, primarily in England. Buttons were imported from Europe and sold to merchants, where consumers could buy them in varying quantities (e.g., a dozen, a gross, a bag). While most European and Native peoples purchased manufactured buttons in this period, archaeological evidence from several Native American sites in New England indicate that Native peoples of the region made their own buttons by casting molten lead (some of which was from discarded lead fabric seals) into stone

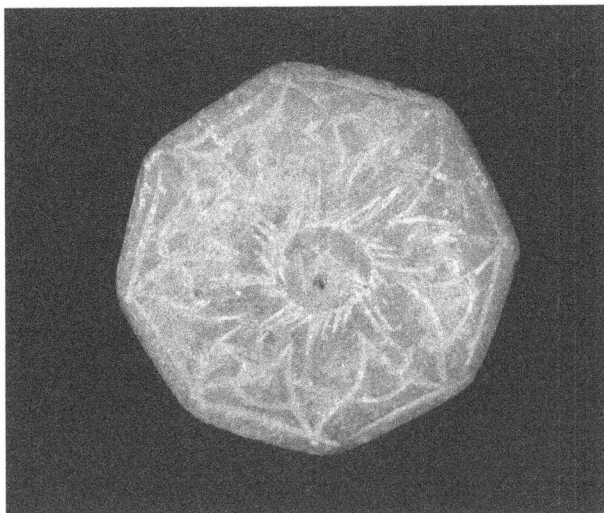

3.5. Octagonal copper-alloy sleeve button, from Old College Cellar, Harvard Yard, Cambridge, Massachusetts. Courtesy of President and Fellows of Harvard College, Peabody Museum of Archaeology and Ethnology, 987-22-10/100223.

molds. Figure 3.4 offers an example of such a button mold from Lincoln, Massachusetts.

Although both Native Americans and the English used stone molds in the early colonial period to cast lead objects, most archaeologically recovered stone molds for buttons are from Native American contexts (Barber 1984; Loren 2007a: 93–94; Willoughby 1935:243–244). Buttons were made in these molds by melting lead or other metal that was poured into the one-part molds, which were usually made of slate (Hinks 1988:60). Elsewhere I have discussed the importance of the stone button mold in the lives of colonial Native American people living in the region that colonists named New England (Loren 2007a:95). Here, however, I wish to focus on a commonly used eighteenth-century button: the octagonal copper-alloy sleeve button with impressed designs (see Figure 3.5).

As White (2005:61) notes, sleeve buttons are easily recognizable when found intact. Sleeve buttons, or cuff links as they are commonly known today, consist of two small buttons joined together by metal links served to hold together the cuffs of shirts while at the same time adding a bit of style to the individual's attire (White 2005:61–62). Sleeve buttons were manufactured during the colonial period in England and France and later in North America. They were octagonal, oval, and round in shape and were cast from a variety of materials, including copper alloys and gold, silver, pewter, copper, and brass (Kent 2001:640; White 2005:61). The etching on sleeve buttons ranges from ornate motifs (as shown here) to less-well-executed designs (White 2005:61). Octagonal sleeve buttons were very popular during the eighteenth century and were widely distributed throughout North America (White 2005:61). Because sleeve buttons could be transferred from one shirt to another, they were carefully curated, and it would be rare to find a person of modest social status with more than one set.

Not surprisingly, small octagonal sleeve buttons have been recovered from numerous English and French sites in eastern North America. The sleeve button in Figure 3.5 was recovered from the same late seventeenth/early eighteenth-century context as the lead fabric seal depicted in Figure 3.3: the cellar hole of Harvard's Old College. Almost identical sleeve buttons have been recovered from colonial Williamsburg and from the Bennett's Point (18QU28) site, a colonial-period tobacco plantation located in Queen Anne's County, Maryland (Baumgarten 2002:159; Maryland Archaeological Conservation Lab 2007; Noël Hume 1973).

Each of the contexts in which this kind of sleeve button was recovered suggests a different kind of dress. Colonial Harvard was known for more somber dress, while artifacts of clothing and adornment recovered from Colonial Williamsburg and Bennett's Point suggest that individuals living within these communities wore more flamboyant fashions (Baumgarten 2002; Maryland Archaeological Conservation Lab 2007).

Octagonal sleeve buttons have been recovered from other contexts as well that suggest varied uses of these small items. For example, they have been recovered from the African Burial Ground National Monument, a cemetery where more than 400 enslaved and free African men, women, and children were buried during the seventeenth and eighteenth centuries outside the boundaries of the settlement of New Amsterdam, now Lower Manhattan (African Burial Ground 2008). Bianchi and Bianco (2006:306) note that clothing fasteners made from metal, bone, and wood were found in direct association with approximately 8 percent of the burials in the archaeologically excavated portion of the cemetery. Six individuals were buried with sleeve buttons. In three burials, sleeve buttons were recovered from near the wrist of the individual, suggesting that the sleeve buttons were used to close the shirtsleeves the individual was wearing at the time of interment. Two sets of cast copper-alloy sleeve buttons very similar to those recovered from Harvard Yard were recovered at the African Burial Ground from the interment of a 40- to 50-year-old man, one near each wrist (Bianchi and Bianco 2006:343).

However, most sleeve buttons found at the site were deposited in ways that suggest that they were used for ornamentation rather than as closures. For example, in the three other burials from which sleeve buttons were recovered, they were in association with other parts of the body (Bianchi and Bianco 2006:310). Two turquoise enamel sleeve button faces associated with an adult woman (Burial 371) might not have been used to fasten a garment, as they were located beneath her left upper arm. In the burial of an adult man (Burial 392), the sleeve buttons were located near the neck of the individual (Bianchi and Bianco 2006:31). The locations of these sleeve buttons suggest that they were not worn to close the cuffs of a shirt but were used in a different way, perhaps not as a clothing attachment but rather as an object of adornment. Additionally, because sleeve buttons are almost always linked to the dress of colonial men (White 2005:57), the use of sleeve buttons in the clothing or adornment of an adult African woman at the time of her burial challenges our expectations of how such items were used in the daily lives of colonial peoples. Such uses open our eyes to new interpretative possibilities, not only as to the use of buttons as adornment in colonial African American contexts but also to unexpected uses of items of adornment in the larger colonial world.

Other examples of buttons used purely as ornamentation rather than being used for function redound through Native American ethnographic collections. Buttons of various sizes, styles, and colors are found woven into baskets and threaded with glass beads in earrings. Without evidence of where an item was placed on or near the body, as in the case of the African Burial Ground, information about how these items were used often eludes us in archaeological analysis. Buttons recovered from excavations are frequently interpreted as items that were lost from an item of clothing. As these examples indicate, sleeve buttons and buttons were used in at least two ways: to help enclose the body and to ornament the body. Octagonal sleeve buttons are a common find in the archaeological record of colonial America, and the interpretation of these items rarely goes beyond mentioning that they were a common, reasonably priced manufactured item that was available nearly everywhere in colonial America. Yet the evidence in this chapter suggests that they were used for more than one fashion and by more than one category of individual.

Tattooing, cloth, and buttons as well as eyeglasses, shoes, shirts, and trousers served to cover naked flesh. They also protected the body from numerous dangers, environmental or sensual. These practices were not only a concern for the colonial period but carried into centuries long after the American Revolution. Consider the design and fashion of middle- and upper-class women's clothing during the Victorian period. It was not enough to simply cover one's body; tight, corseted waists, expansive skirts, and narrow shoulders were purposely constructed to limit movement and protect the body (Davis 1994: 98; Entwistle 2000:163–164). Not only did these constricting fashions limit the amount a woman could eat at one sitting (a pleasure of the flesh) but they also prevented her body from doing activities such as housework, which disallowed middle- and upper-class women from being in contact with unhygienic environments (Entwistle 2000:162–163). Victorian dress reform in the nineteenth century critiqued restrictive dress and promoted new, freer fashions that included bloomers in lieu of skirts and union suits in lieu of corsets; fashions that were then critiqued, not surprisingly, for enabling sexual impropriety and social liberty (Entwistle 2000:164–165).

In the next chapter, I investigate some examples of adornments that were added to the body. Rather than just surface embellishment, adornments were an integral part of dress, an extension of the body that influenced dress, style, and even how someone could move through a social space. Adornments were both secular and sacred and were laid on the surface of the tattooed, marked, or clothed body to express aspects of social identity.

Notes

1. Not all seals were used for cloth. Other items were often marked with lead seals, including red paint brought to North America for trade with Native peoples (Gregory 1980:78–80).

4

~ ✤ ~

Attaching Adornments

Know, first, who you are; and then adorn yourself accordingly.
—Epictetus

While it could be argued that artifacts used to adorn the body go beyond what is absolutely necessary for survival, in some ways many objects used for ornamentation are as important to the body as clothing itself (Burton 2001:27). Adornments temporarily transform the body (Steiner 1990). Consider how leaders and chiefs often don their best regalia for political events and include adornments such as presidential medals to publicly display their knowledge and authority to their audience. These adornments are integral to the sartorial presentation of the self and are difficult to identify as a separate category.

Adornment is also used to add to the body to create meaning, and it is often the case that items of adornment had different meanings for their users than they did for their producers. For example, the archaeological work on glass beads recovered from the Spanish colonial communities of St. Augustine and Pensacola has suggested that beads were used not only as jewelry but also for rosaries and particularly (in certain contexts) as amulets and magical protection for women (Deagan 2002). These uses point to people's active manipulation of adornment and to how the meaning of adornments is contingent on context. The objects of adornment under consideration in this chapter are glass beads, crucifixes, and pierced coins.

Examples of colonial adornments derive from European, African, Native American, and multiethnic contexts. Whether they were secular or sacred, adornment practices were an important visual constituent of colonial identity. Although objects of adornment are not exactly numerous at all colonial sites, they are often recovered from sites throughout North America. They include items such as jewelry, beads, hair combs, and religious medals. For example, at the Stobo Plantation site in South Carolina, adornment artifacts represent a very small percentage of the assemblage (just over 1 percent) (Zierdan 2002:192–194). But the adornment artifacts that were recovered from this eighteenth-century rice plantation are notable. A silver cane tip indicated that when James Stobo presented himself in the community he did so with style (Zierdan 2002:192). Yet a brass finger ring set with a glass stone engraved with a crucifix did not belong to Stobo, a strident dissident who deplored the Catholic Church, and researchers of the site were left to wonder who could have deposited this ring. Could it have been owned by enslaved Africans living on the plantation who were devout Catholics, or was it owned by Christianized Indians from the Apalachee province? As Zierden suggests (2002:195), although we may never know the provenance of this object, the object is important as a signature of colonialism, the meeting of diverse cultural beliefs and ideologies. This ring is also emblematic of the practices of dress during the colonial period. Colonial peoples in North America built upon familiar adornment practices but combined objects of adornment on the body in ways that were unique to the context of colonial America.

Capturing the Sky: Nueva Cadiz Glass Beads

Glass beads first arrived in North America from production sites in Italy and Amsterdam and other areas of Europe and were some of the first items to be traded with the indigenous peoples. They soon became one of the most common European-manufactured items related to clothing and adornment in North America and other parts of the globe during the colonial period. Glass beads were produced in a multitude of colors and forms that included very small beads (sometimes described as seed beads), very large beads made of blown glass; beads wound with wire; drawn, pressed and molded beads; and etched beads. They were produced in almost every conceivable color or color combination.

As a commodity and an item with meaning, glass beads have reached almost an iconic status within material studies in historical archaeology. Quimby (1966) detailed the occurrence of glass beads on early colonial-period sites throughout the Great Lakes. Kidd and Kidd's (1970) typology of glass beads brought new understandings of the construction and composition of beads to archaeological analysis, while Karklins (1985, 1992), Hamell

(1983), Phillips (1998), and Turgeon (2001, 2004) discuss the use and meaning of glass beads for Native peoples in Canada and the Eastern Woodlands. This research on the chronology and sourcing of glass beads has provided a solid baseline for current discussions of the use and meaning of glass beads in Native American contexts, particularly for the current emphasis on the use of different bead forms. Color has also been an important component of this research on Native American contexts (see especially Hamell 1983) and has also been a central concept in discussions of glass beads recovered from African American sites (Singleton 2005; Thomas 2002; Wilkie 1995, 1997).

Recent scholarly interest has focused on how Native peoples incorporated glass beads into adornment and embroidery practices throughout the colonial Eastern Woodlands and on the complex meanings glass beads carried in those contexts (e.g., Karklins 1985, 1992; Phillips 1998; Turgeon 2001, 2004, 2006). Laurier Turgeon eloquently argues that material culture placed on the body becomes part of one's body:

> Food and clothing are integrated into or put onto the body and thereby transform it. . . . A piece of clothing is more than a sign, or a representation of something, it is an essence in itself. This material association between biological (the body) and cultural domains is what makes alimentary and vestimentary practices so efficient for the affirmation of individual and collective identities (Turgeon 2006:108).

Turgeon (2004:35–36) has argued that glass beads were a particularly important aspect of colonial dress because of the associations between beads and bodies, particularly because beads were often associated with eyes or light. Thus, when an individual wore beads on the body, they were an important visual aspect of how that person constructed his or her identity. Light is captured in glass and this translucence was unique among much colonial-period material culture. As Turgeon (2004:35) reminds us, "The polished surface of beads conveyed the notions of finish, brilliance, aliveness, and action." In many northeastern Native American communities during the early colonial period, glass beads were metaphors for vision and visibility (Turgeon 2004:36). Among many Native American communities, glass beads were initially worn as jewelry, but soon they were incorporated into other items, such as the bag seen in Figure 4.1.

In the archaeological record, we rarely have a complete beaded object to use as the basis for a discussion of beading practices. Usually glass beads

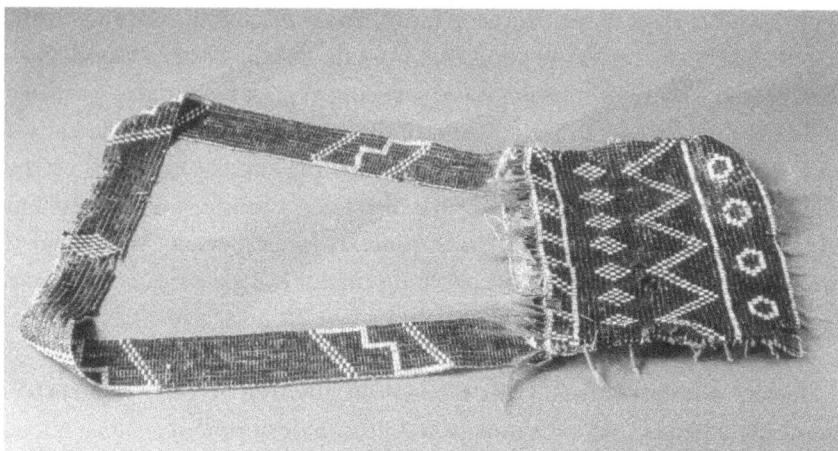

4.1. Shot bag of glass beads with tinklers, eighteenth century, Quebec. Courtesy of President and Fellows of Harvard College, Peabody Museum of Archaeology and Ethnology, 67-10-10/288.

are recovered as single objects, and interpretations tend to focus on analysis based on chronology. Archaeological research that examines how glass beads were used in practices of clothing and adornment based on where beads are located in relation to human remains has also provided some detail (e.g., Loren 2007a). Additionally, ethnographic collections provide numerous examples of how glass beads were sewn onto clothing, woven into belts, embroidered on bags, worn as necklaces and earrings, woven into hair, and hung from cradle boards (Karklins 1992:12–13; Neitzel 1965:88–89; Pietak 1998). One example of this use of glass beads is the eighteenth-century bag manufactured in Quebec shown in Figure 4.1. At first glance, the bag appears to be made from wampum. A closer examination, however, reveals that the bag is constructed using cut dark ultramarine and white glass beads woven in a geometric design commonly used in wampum belts. The back of the bag is composed of blue stroud with metal tinklers sewn along the edges. The ingenuity used to create this object suggests more than simply exchanging one material for another. The glass beads on this item, while mimicking wampum, have a translucence and luster not found in shell beads, indicating that the raw material itself had value to the beader that shell beads did not.

With these concepts in mind, I want to focus on a specific type of glass bead found on seventeenth-century colonial sites in North America: the

Nueva Cadiz bead. Nueva Cadiz is the modern name for a particular type of tubular drawn-glass bead produced during the sixteenth century; it was identified by John Goggin (Deagan 2002:12, 57). These beads, which were made of both turquoise and darker blue glass, were produced in two forms: straight and twisted. Because of the limited period of production, Nueva Cadiz beads are extremely diagnostic and are used to date early colonial-period sites in North and South America. A variety of Nueva Cadiz beads that were shorter and smaller than those usually defined as Nueva Cadiz were produced in the late sixteenth and early seventeenth centuries, indicating a brief renaissance of this bead type (Lapham 2001). Nueva Cadiz and Nueva Cadiz–like beads have been mostly commonly associated with Spanish colonial sites. However, these beads have been recovered from other colonial contexts, including Seneca sites in New York, Susquehannock sites in Pennsylvania, Iroquois sites in southern Ontario, and Native American contexts in Wisconsin. (Ellis and Ferris 1990; Fitzgerald 1982; Kent 1983; Kenyon 1982; Lapham 2001; Smith and Graybill 1977; Sempowski 1994; Wray 1983; Wray et al. 1991). The string of glass beads shown in Figure 4.2 was recovered from a Native American site in Wisconsin.

The majority of sites mentioned here are Native American contexts, yet Lapham (2001) discusses an assemblage of Nueva Cadiz–like beads recovered from the early English colony of Jamestown. Established in 1607, Jamestown was located on the banks of the James River 60 miles from the mouth of the Chesapeake Bay and approximately 15 miles from the Powhatan community of Werowocomoco, which was the center of the Powhatan Confederacy (Gallivan 2003, 2004). Beginning in 1994, a major archaeological program known as the Jamestown Rediscovery Archaeology Project has worked to recover much of the early fort, the remains of several houses and wells, the graves of several of the early settlers, and thousands of early seventeenth-century artifacts (Kelso et al. 1997, 1999; Mallios 2000). During the early years of the Jamestown settlement, the Powhatan Confederacy—a polity of 30 Native American communities—was led by Chief Powhatan (Wahunsunacock), an individual who was documented in both historical and popular sources (Gallivan 2003, 2004). The site of Werowocomoco was first located by archaeological survey in the 1970s. Archaeological investigations at the site and collaborative research on the Powhatan Confederacy are conducted by the Werowocomoco Research Group (Gallivan 2003, 2004; Gallivan et al. 2006).

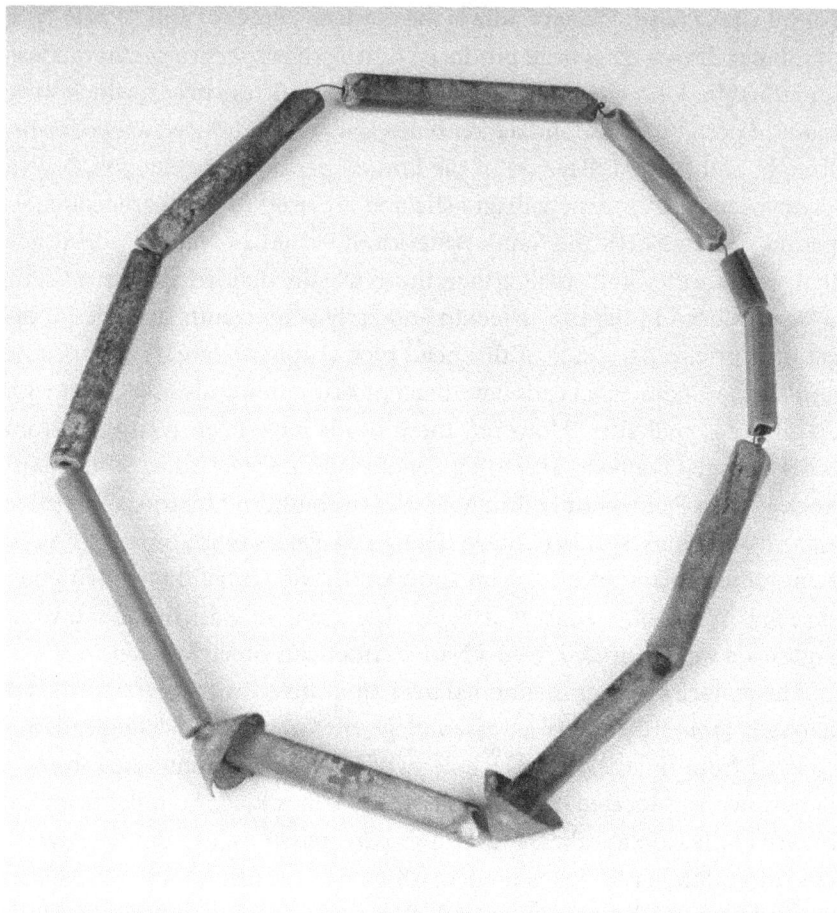

4.2. Conical copper beads and Nueva Cadiz glass beads, seventeenth century, Wisconsin. Museum documentation indicates that beads are "as originally strung." Courtesy of President and Fellows of Harvard College, Peabody Museum of Archaeology and Ethnology, 21-15-10/92461.

Lapham (2001) notes that the Nueva Cadiz–like beads recovered from Jamestown are a later variety of Nueva Cadiz beads that were produced in the sixteenth and seventeenth centuries. At 18 percent of the total bead assemblage at the site, this type of bead occurs in much greater quantities at Jamestown than any at other site in the Middle Atlantic and northeastern regions. The Nueva Cadiz–like turquoise beads recovered from Jamestown are smaller than those recovered from other contemporaneous sites. Additionally, a navy blue variety recovered at the site appears to be unique to Jamestown Island. Lapham (2001:5) indicates that "differences between Nueva Cadiz-like beads unearthed at Jamestown and those found elsewhere in the Middle Atlantic and Northeast attest to the uniqueness of the two Jamestown varieties and to their affinity with 16th-century Spanish types."

Lapham's research focuses on assessing the origin of and chronology for the beads recovered from Jamestown. But how were these beads used at Jamestown? Should we assume that the Nueva Cadiz–like beads recovered from the site were used only for trade with Powhatans living in the neighboring community of Werowocomoco? Gallivan and colleagues (2006:33) note that socioeconomic relations between Jamestown and Werowocomoco were established through the exchange of "food for items with symbolic resonance (including copper and glass beads) and those with practical uses (including swords and iron tools)." John Smith, perhaps one of the most well-known English visitors at Werowocomoco, was known to have traded numerous blue glass beads to Powhatan individuals, and these glass beads were fit into aspects of Powhatan color symbolism (Gallivan et al. 2006:34). In *The generall historie of Virginia*, John Smith provided this account of an exchange with Chief Powhatan:

> [Smith] glanced in the eyes of Powhatan many trifles, who fixed his humor upon a few blew beades. A long time he importunately desired them, but Smith seemed so much the more to affect them, as being composed of a most rare substance of the coulour of the skyes, and not to be worne but by the greatest kings in the world. This made him halfe madde to be the owner of such strange Jewells: so that ere we departed, for a pound or two of blew beades, he brought over my king for 2 or 300 Bushells of corne; yet parted good friends (Smith 1624:108).

Presumably, the Nueva Cadiz–like beads recovered from Jamestown were to be used not in the dressing practices of English colonists but rather for trade with local Powhatans. Hundreds of round blue glass beads have been recovered from both Jamestown and Werowocomoco, yet no Nueva Cadiz or Nueva Cadiz–like beads have been recovered from Werowocomoco (Gallivan et al. 2006). What accounts for this? It may be that Powhatans were just not interested in the shape of Nueva Cadiz beads and chose round glass beads over this tubular variety. This explanation would account for the fact that tubular glass beads have been recovered at Jamestown. But it is possible that Nueva Cadiz–like beads were worn by members of the Jamestown community?

Francis (1988:2, 30–31) and Turgeon (2004:27) argue that Europeans placed little economic value on beads, desiring instead gems and gold and silver jewelry. This sentiment is captured in the 1624 quote above, where Smith calls glass beads "trinkets." Such historical quotes ground the reasoning of Francis, Turgeon, and others that glass beads were rarely worn by people of European descent in North America and that they were highly valued and used only by people of African and Native American descent. People of European descent did wear and use glass beads, but most forms recognized by scholars as those worn and used in North America are jet (for rosaries), crystal, and small cut-glass beads used for embroidery on clothing and altar cloths (Deagan 2002:38–40; White 2005:81–83; Malischke 2009:32–34). Glass beads outside of these categories are usually associated with non-European people in different colonial contexts.

These kinds of interpretations, however, narrow the range of interpretive possibilities for the use of glass beads as adornment. We know that some glass beads (including varieties that are assumed to be "made for trade") were incorporated into larger pieces of jewelry and were even worn as necklaces by European women of modest means, such as servants, chambermaids, and valets who could not afford more expensive forms of jewelry (Turgeon 2004:27; see also White 2005:81–83). With this information in mind, is it so difficult to imagine that in the struggling community of seventeenth-century Jamestown (and even with John Smith's judgment of glass beads as "trifles"), those wishing to decorate their bodies would follow the lead of their Powhatan neighbors and include glass beads as part of their practices of adornment? And that this practice may have occurred in other colonial regions where people of European descent emulated Native and African neighbors to wear glass beads as adornment and, in so doing, actively created new identities in colonial North America?

Attaching Christ: Crucifixes and Other Religious Adornments

Perhaps there is no more powerful emblem of conversion to Christianity than the crucifix. The crucifix depicts Christ's body at the moment of death. Worn on the body, this image symbolizes the metaphorical submission of self (both the physical body and the soul) to God. Deagan (2002: 38) notes that when used in a Catholic context, crucifixes and other religious items "are not considered to be charms, amulets or idols but rather are tangible reminders to Catholics of their faith, religious duties, and rewards." During the period when Christian missionaries were attempting to convert souls in the New World, especially during the seventeenth and eighteenth centuries, they distributed crucifixes and other religious paraphernalia among Native American populations to allow individuals to visually denote their conversion as an attachment on the body. Native peoples in the Americas resisted attempts to convert them in varying degrees, depending on the group being converted and those attempting the conversion. Nevertheless, crucifixes and other religious ornaments are common at many seventeenth- and eighteenth-century sites, particularly mission contexts.

During the seventeenth century, numerous places of worship and conversion were established in the American colonies, including several praying towns in New England and numerous Catholic missions in New France, New Amsterdam, and New Spain. The first missions in present-day New Mexico (then part of New Spain) were established after 1598. During the next 100 years, Franciscan priests founded more than 40 additional missions, most of them along the Rio Grande (Weber 1994:94–97; see also Lightfoot 2004). Among these was the seventeenth-century mission established among the Hopi at Awatovi.

One of the more interesting contexts relating to the incorporation of religious symbols into the lives of Native peoples are those that were recovered by archaeologists at the site of the Pueblo Revolt (Pruecel 2002). In 1680, following 82 years of colonization, the Pueblo Indians of New Mexico rose up against the Spanish Crown and its arm of oppression—the Church. During the Pueblo Revolt, 401 Spanish colonists and 21 Franciscan missionaries were killed (Pruecel 2002; Wilcox 2002). Following the revolt, Pueblo peoples were able to revitalize their traditional religion. They "revived their traditional ceremonies, rebuilt their kivas, and reconsecrated their shrines" (Pruecel 2002:3). For Pueblo people, the crucifix was the mark of Spanish oppression (Figure 4.3). The archaeological record shows that they reinterpreted crosses and crucifixes and incorporated them into kiva art and ceramics. They also included them in several burials.

Mobley-Tanaka (2002) argues that during the period of Spanish colonization prior to the Pueblo Revolt, Pueblo artists incorporated crosses into their ceramics, jewelry, and mural paintings not as a mark of religious conversion but rather as a symbol intended to misinform Spanish viewers. During the period of Spanish colonization prior to the revolt, the cross

4.3. Part of Jeddito black-on-yellow pottery bowl, Awatovi, Antelope Mesa, Arizona, ca. 1629–1700. Courtesy of President and Fellows of Harvard College, Peabody Museum of Archaeology and Ethnology, 35-126-10/5560A.

replaced a stylistically similar mark for dragonflies and birds in flight that existed on Pueblo pottery prior to colonization; the similarity of these two symbols made it possible for the Pueblo peoples to silently infuse meaningful images into Spanish-controlled places. Liebmann (2002) provides evidence that Pueblo artists continued to incorporate and transform Christian imagery into their discourse of resistance as they formulated their identities following the Pueblo Revolt. In his analysis of a drawing located on the wall of a Pueblo village occupied during or just after the revolt or reconquest, Liebmann discusses how Pueblos resisted Spanish colonization through the inversion of Spanish images. An image on the wall depicts a figure with a halo that strongly resembles European depictions of the Virgin Mary, saints, and the Holy Trinity. Other aspects of the image—the points in the halo and two concentric circles surrounding the face—also suggest the incorporation of traditional Pueblo art. The image is thus a combination of Christian and Pueblo imagery and is indicative of strategies used to preserve culture and recreate Pueblo identities; it allowed for active, explicit resistance rather than the passive forms of resistance found in the use of crosses prior to the revolt (Liebmann 2002).

A similar strategy of identity manipulation is discussed by Elizabeth Bollwerk (2006), who offers an interesting example of how Native peoples

strategically used Christian symbols during the nineteenth century. Bollwerk outlines how Potawatomi chief Leopold Pokagon employed a form
of "selective consumerism" in his Michigan village during the early part of
the nineteenth century that enabled him to control the types of European-
manufactured goods that were entering his community (see also Wagner
1998). Chief Pokagon and Pokagon band members allied themselves with
Catholic missionaries rather than with the Baptist ministers who lived
nearby. They did this only for religious reasons but also because it created
an important political alliance during the band's struggle to avoid removal
from tribal homelands. In 1830, Pokagon and other band members were
baptized by the vicar general of the Detroit Diocese, and soon after a mission was established to serve the Pokagon Potawatomi. This affiliation with
the Catholic Church created a new identity for the Potawatomi of the St. Joseph River Valley; thereafter they were known as the Pokagon Band of Potawatomi Indians (Bollwerk 2006). The St. Benedict medal recovered from
the Pokagon Village site (20BE13) and a portrait of Chief Pokagon wearing
a crucifix are the material remnants of these complex relationships—the
subtle, purposeful manipulations through which Pokagon band members
physically presented themselves as converted in a way that enabled them to
keep their land.

Crucifixes and other religious objects are the residues of the attempts
of missionaries to spread a religious ideology in the New World, a central
goal for many colonizers, especially France and Spain. Many Native peoples
incorporated Christianity into their lives, resulting in an important shift
in their worldviews. Yet one wonders if the categories of "converted" and
"unconverted" adequately capture the complexity of the identity negotia-
tions Native peoples made. When religious ornaments are recovered from
colonial-period Native American sites they commonly are interpreted as
evidence of missionary activity, perhaps even to as evidence that the Native peoples had converted to Christianity (see Larsen et al. 2001; McEwan
1993, 2001; Thomas 1993). But does the presence of both numerous Christian symbols (saint medals, crucifixes, etc.) and Native American religious
elements signify that the owner of these items was on his or her way to
becoming a convert? Or should we perhaps reflect on how Native Americans wore Christian symbols in combination with other Native American
and European clothing and adornment? Here we must be aware of the
limitations of functional categories; Christian symbols can indicate more
than religious expression or conversion. The context in which a Christian

symbol was worn is crucial; in different contexts it may have simultaneously spoken to other issues such as ethnicity, status, or gender. Was it used as a reminder of faith or used as a charm or amulet? Crucifixes and religious medals held certain meanings for baptized individuals, but rosary beads and other Christian symbols took on new meanings when Native American men, women, and children publicly combined these objects with indigenous items to purposefully and publicly negotiate self in the context of religious conversion.

An example of the complicated use of religious symbols in a colonial context is found at Presidio Los Adaes, the capital of Spanish Texas from 1729 to 1770. Los Adaes was situated along the eastern border of eighteenth-century Spanish Texas, just miles from French Louisiana. The presidio was occupied by Spanish and mixed-blood military personnel and their families as well as civilian settlers from New Spain, French refugees, Caddo Indians, and some escaped African slaves from French Louisiana (Avery 1995; Loren 2001a; Loren 2007b; Gregory 1984; Gregory et al. 2004). I have discussed the meaningful manipulations of clothing and adornment in this multiethnic colonial community elsewhere (Loren 2007b); here I want to focus on the religious items recovered from one house at the site and how they may have been used by the population.

A structure referred to as the "Southeast Structure," located southeast of the main presidio building, featured a large outdoor kitchen. In 1982, H. F. "Pete" Gregory excavated the structure and recovered numerous artifacts of clothing and adornment: four fabric seals, a scrap of gold lace, a piece of blue-gray woven fabric, collar ornaments for military shirts, a copper brooch, an earring, rings, numerous large and seed glass beads, patterned buckles and buttons, and three tinkler cones (Gregory 1984). The variety of clothing and adornment artifacts found among the households suggests that the occupants creatively configured their dress by combining aspects of European-style fashion, evidenced by the blue-gray wool, patterned shoe buckles, and collar ornaments, with aspects of Native American–style dress, evidenced by the glass seed beads and tinkler cones that were likely sewn onto buckskin clothing (Loren 2001a, 2007b).

The religious ornaments recovered from the household add to the dynamic fashion embodied at the presidio and indicate how religious adornments and amulets were used to promote physical as well as spiritual well-being. A large brass St. John of Matha medal and a smaller Holy

Family medal recovered from the household were likely worn with glass bead necklaces and copper-alloy rings, brooches, and earrings. Amulets, the focus of the next section, were believed to possess magical powers and were also worn in combination with religious items and other items of adornment. Numerous metal *higas* (amulets in the shape of a closed fist worn to ward off the evil eye and promote health) were recovered from the household, suggesting that residents were anxious about the health of both their souls and their physical bodies (Gregory 1984; see also Deagan 2002). Gregory et al. (2009) postulate based on a peculiar set of artifacts recovered from a cooking pit that one of the house's occupants was a *curandera*, or folk healer. A brass wick trimmer, egg shell fragments, and tubular red glass beads were found close to the St. John of Matha medal at the bottom of the pit. In *curanderismo*, which includes elements derived from both indigenous and Spanish cultures, a female healer prays for spiritual cleaning and protection against evil spirits. Among the items commonly used by a *curandera* are eggs, candles, pictures of saints, animal bones, herbs, and holy water (Gregory et al. 2009), items that closely resemble those recovered from the cooking pit. The combination of Catholic medals with secular items and amulets found at this household in colonial New Spain indicate how aspects of Catholicism and its associated material culture were woven not only into worldviews and identities of people living at Los Adaes but also into body adornment practices.

Attaching Protection: Pierced Coins

Individuals in many colonial contexts commonly used a variety of strategies to protect their physical and mental bodies. For example, although shoes were obviously used to enclose the feet, in eighteenth-century Massachusetts, European colonists also used them to protect the body in other ways. During a 2008 renovation to the eighteenth-century Hancock-Clarke house located in Lexington, researchers found shoes in the walls and above the doorways of the structure (Lexington Historical Society 2007; see also Stephens 2010). St. George documents how people placed shoes and other items above doorways of New England homes or buried them beneath the hearth in order to protect the people living in the house from the dangers of the outside world and from maleficent bodies (St. George 1998:188–193). In this way, Puritans assigned magical properties to everyday items. As another example, they filled Bellarmine bottles with urine, hair, and pins to make them into "witch bottles" as a strategy to keep evil spirits away.

These items used to protect the body, oftentimes worn on the body itself, differ from religious medals or crucifixes in that they are not "used as intermediaries between their owner and a higher power" (Deagan 2002:87). Rather, these items are invested with meanings and beliefs that imbue them with power, sometimes magical in nature but always protective of the physical body. Items used as amulets or charms fall into two categories: those specifically made for protection (such as horns or *higas* to ward off the evil eye) and everyday items put into use as charms or amulets (such as shoes or pierced coins). In this section, I describe some examples of the use of pierced coins to protect the physical body.

Puritans were not the only people that wanted to guard their physical bodies. A variety of strategies to protect the body were used in other colonial sites in North America. Kathleen Deagan (2002:87–105) provides a lengthy list of amulets recovered from Spanish colonial sites in the Southeast, all of which were intended to protect the wearer from illness or to help the individual withstand or bring about certain bodily processes: teething, nosebleeds, hemorrhage, or conception. These practices of using protective adornments often derived from European homelands. Native and African peoples in North America during the eighteenth and nineteenth centuries also pierced or drilled holes in coins and thimbles for the purpose of adornment. African Americans' use of pierced coins in adornment practices during the late eighteenth and nineteenth centuries is often related to the folk use of charms to ward off evil spirits or illness (Davidson 2004:23; Wilkie 1995). At the Dog River Plantation located in Mobile, Alabama, an 1840 Liberty silver dime recovered from the site may be an example of such a belief system at work (Waselkov and Gums 2000:166).

Davidson (2004) outlines this kind of practice in his discussion of the presence of pierced coins at an African American cemetery in use in Dallas during the period 1869–1907. He (2004:23) notes that pierced American coins were recovered from 15 interments, usually from the neck or ankle region. To trace the origin of this practice among African Americans in the South, Davidson reviewed narratives of former slaves gathered by the Works Progress Administration in the 1930s and folklore collections related to the use of coins as charms (Davidson 2004:23–26). The practice was common among African Americans in Dallas and other areas of the South

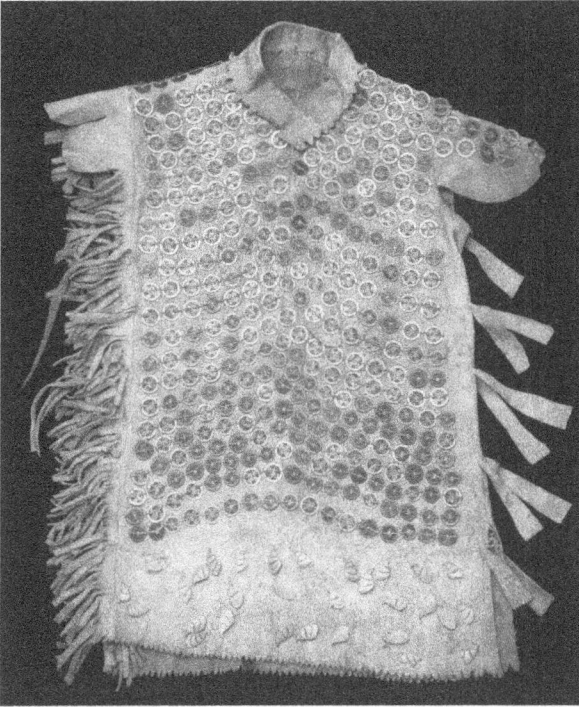

4.4. Walrus-skin coat with puffin beaks and Chinese coins, Tlingit, eighteenth century. Courtesy of President and Fellows of Harvard College, Peabody Museum of Archaeology and Ethnology, 69-30-10/2065.

during the nineteenth and early twentieth centuries, when coins were used as charms to ward off evil or protect against health risks. Pierced coins were placed around the necks of young children for protection during teething and weaning, and adults apparently wore them to ward off rheumatism and other ailments (Davidson 2004:37–45).

While pierced coins found within late-eighteenth- and nineteenth-century African American contexts have been related to religious or spiritual practices, the same cannot be said for pierced coins found within Native Alaskan contexts. Too often, the Chinese coins incorporated into Tlingit and other Northwest Coast Indian clothing has not been examined in terms of its use as a charm related to a religious practice. Rather, this material been interpreted as similar to brass tinkler cones or brass janglers used in other kinds of Native American clothing practices. For example, coins minted with perforations that were used as adornment or charms can be found on the late-eighteenth-century Tlingit armor shown in Figure 4.4, which is covered with Chinese coins from the reigns of four consecutive emperors: Shun-Zhi (A.D. 1644–1661), Kang-Xi (A.D. 1662–1722), Yong-Zhen (A.D. 1722–1735), and Qian-Long (A.D. 1735–1796). In this case, the coins used on the armor protected the body of the wearer in multiple ways: coins were particularly effective when worn as armor, and the coins that adorned armor in war and ceremonial settings symbolized the status of warrior (Henrickson 2008; see also Wolf 1982:187).

And what of pierced coins recovered from predominately European contexts? Pierced coins have been recovered from Jamestown (Kelso et al. 1997; Mallios 2000:42–43). Kelso and colleagues (1997:48; 1999:11) suggest that English settlers pierced coins to make items for trade with neighboring Native peoples—that in this frontier place, coins were more valuable as jewelry for barter with Native peoples than as legal tender. These kinds of discussions, however, need to take into account the facts that coin charms were commonly used in many parts of Europe from the fourteenth through the nineteenth centuries (Davidson 2004:26, 29–30; Hill 2007) and that this practice was also followed by people of European descent living in colonial America.

While researching past excavations conducted in Harvard Yard as part of our continuing research on colonial Harvard, my colleagues and I were surprised to find that one of the three coins recovered from previous excavations—a seventeenth-century Richmond farthing issued between 1625 and 1635—was pierced and was likely worn as an adornment (Figure 4.5). Our surprise was not because the coin was pierced, as pierced coins are commonly recovered from colonial contexts, but because this was the first evidence of such items in the context of seventeenth-century Harvard.

In colonial New England, Puritans viewed flamboyant fashion as disorderly. Bay Colony sumptuary laws loudly enforced a modest and conservative style of dress among all inhabitants; a style that would indicate at a glance who a person was by what he or she wore (De Marly 1990:35–38; Goodwin 1999:112). In 1651, the members of the Massachusetts legislature had declared their "utter detestation and dislike, that men or women of mean condition, should take upon them the garb of Gentlemen, by wearing Gold or Silver Lace, or Buttons, or Points at their knees, or to walk in great Boots (quoted in Degler 1984:11). Not surprisingly, the 1655 Harvard College Laws mirrored this orthodox vision of conservative dress, dictating that students were not permitted to leave their chambers without "Coate, Gowne, or Cloake" and that "every one, everywhere shall weare modest and somber habit, without strange ruffianlike or Newfangled fashions, without all lavishe dress, or excesse of Apparell whatsoever" (Colonial Society of Massachusetts 1935:330).

4.5. Pierced coin, seventeenth century, Harvard Yard, Cambridge, Massachusetts. Courtesy of President and Fellows of Harvard College, Peabody Museum of Archaeology and Ethnology, 987-22-10/100153.

Artifacts of clothing and adornment recovered from the fill of the Old College cellar that date to the late seventeenth century (1680–1700) include four metal hook-and-eye clasps, a bone button, a copper-alloy button with embossed decoration, one iron knee buckle, several lead fabric seals (most likely from bales of woolen fabric), and a pierced Richmond farthing (Stubbs 1992:553–554, 558). This modest assemblage suggests that the students likely followed prescribed institutional fashions. The only item that suggests otherwise is the pierced Richmond farthing. Even though college laws did not prohibit the wearing of coins as jewelry, this practice did not comply with "somber habit." The pierced coin recovered from the Old College cellar suggests that the wearer was anxious about bodily protection, even witchcraft, while being educated at a Puritan institution, where he was being rigorously schooled in knowledge about hellfire, brimstone, God's wrath, and the dangers of witchcraft.

Seventeenth-century Harvard was a multicultural setting. For approximately 25 years after the establishment of the Harvard Indian College in 1655, English and Native American youths were trained side by side to become ministers (Lepore 1998:32–38; Morison 1995:129). Does the pierced coin connect us to the Wampanoag and Nipmuc students who were being educated at the college? Does it indicate that some of these students chose to embody practices that were more familiar in their home communities of Mashpee, Aquinnah, and Hassanamesit Woods? We hope that our research at the site will provide more answers, but this pierced coin provides us with insight into how seventeenth-century people at Harvard chose to protect their bodies through adornment. Ongoing research may provide more answers on this object and how it was worn, but for now this pierced coin raises questions about how individuals at seventeenth-century Harvard chose to protect their bodies through adornment that went against the grain of institutional ideals.

Several of the adornment practices discussed in this chapter extend into the nineteenth century, indicating the importance of particular adornment practices for many communities long after they were embodied in colonial contexts. As White (2005:1–2) notes, care must be taken not to marginalize small finds in archaeological interpretation by categorizing them only by their function and not examining the context and meaning that items of adornment may have held for the owner. Items of adornment provide us with an avenue for understanding complex issues of identity and the ways that people chose to embody self (see also Deagan 2002; Loren and Beaudry 2006). In the next chapter, I discuss several assemblages of items of clothing and adornment to outline some of the diverse practices by which dress and identity were constructed in a variety of colonial contexts.

5

~ ❀ ~

Clothed in the Colonial World

Good clothes open all doors.
—Thomas Fuller

When I look at archaeological and ethnographic collections, I am always taken with the fact that each object seems to carry several layers of meaning. Objects such as the Native Alaskan necklace in Figure 5.1 do not fall neatly into categories constructed by my museum predecessors. If this object had been lost, discarded, or buried with its owner, we would have known it in the archaeological record only through its components: faunal remains, a carved ivory needle case, a brass bead, a brass finger a ring, a crucifix, and a Chinese coin. The original strip of leather onto which each item is strung is intact. Because this object is still in it original form, we have an opportunity to interpret the components of the necklace both separately and, more important, in relationship to one another. While the motivation for placing a crucifix on a necklace with a Chinese coin and a small animal skull is unknown, it is clear that the act of making this necklace and wearing it was significant for the owner. Each component of the necklace—the crucifix, the animal bones, the ring, even the brass bead—is a meaningful piece of adornment in its own right, but when layered together each component adds to the power and impact of the necklace when viewed together as one item. In this way the necklace speaks to us about the intent of its maker, how this individual drew from several different cultures to make a necklace intended to be worn in the colonial world.

This necklace is just one visual reminder of the ways in which colonial peoples pulled together different fashions to mediate their place in the colonial world. The diverse ways that colonial peoples expressed themselves through clothing and adornment offer a discourse of identity in the context

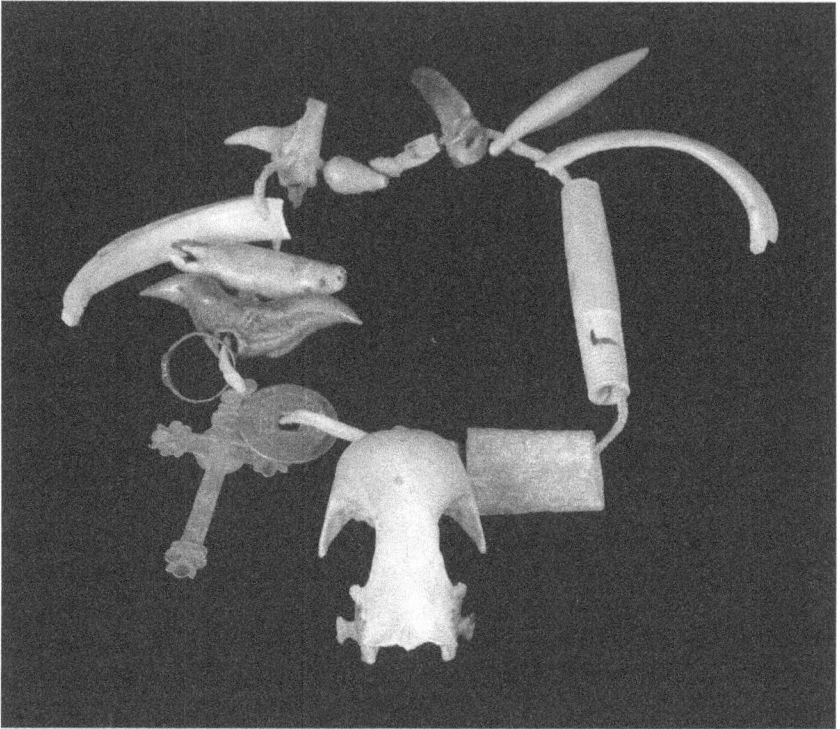

5.1. Necklace of leather thong with bone, animal teeth, ring, metal cross, and coin, nine-teenth century, Northwest Coast. Courtesy of President and Fellows of Harvard College, Peabody Museum of Archaeology and Ethnology, 38-44-10/12889.

of colonial projects that were fraught with regulations, tensions, anxiet-ies, desires, and tastes. While the necklace may have been similar to other objects in colonial America—for example, the octagonal cuff links found in New York and Massachusetts—the ways these objects were used were specific to their context and were meaningful to those who created and then viewed those fashions.

This point is illustrated in the archaeological work that has been done on the clothing and adornment of enslaved Africans and African Americans. Anne Yentsch's (1994) examination of clothing and adornment artifacts recovered from the Calvert site in Annapolis, Maryland, has enabled her to bring forth various stories of dress that have been lost in documentary sources. Glass beads that adorned the necks and wrists of African women and children and clothing fasteners adorned with a hand to protect the wearer from the power of witches have been recovered in the mid-Atlantic colonies in particularly meaningful ensembles (Yentsch 1994:33). Whites dismissed such objects as baubles but allowed African women to use glass beads to express themselves visually (albeit silently). These kinds of dress were a visual discourse, a way to communicate self with those that understood the meaning of such forms of clothing and adornment. Similarly, Alexandra Chan (2007) analyzes items of clothing and adornment recovered in a slave context in Medford, Massachusetts—for example a small stone bead crafted by an enslaved African—in the context of a dialogue between the individuals who occupied Ten Hills Farm: the Isaac Royall family and 63 enslaved individuals of African descent (Chan 2007:93–94, 140). In both of these examples, enslaved Africans wore clothing that was in some sense similar to the clothing worn by those who were enslaving them. But the African Americans constructed their dress using combinations of clothing and adornment that carried multiple layers of meaning.

In this section, I discuss two different assemblages of clothing and adornment artifacts: the first from Dutch New Netherland and the second from French Louisiana. In these examples, I explore the meanings that different combinations of European-manufactured and Native American-manufactured items held and how these objects were part of a social discourse and were mobilized to create specific identities in the colonial world. In the example from Dutch New Netherland, I begin with a relatively small collection of items of clothing and adornment recovered from household contexts, while in the example from French Louisiana I focus on a larger assemblage of clothing and adornment items recovered from domestic and burial contexts. My goal here is to problematize these two assemblages, consider some of the existing stereotypes about the dress of certain colonial peoples, and investigate how disparate practices of dressing the body became intertwined in multiethnic communities.

Clothed in Dutch New Netherland: Burlington Island

In the 1620s, the Dutch government established the colony of New Netherland (Jacobs 2005:35–37). The first settlers arrived in early 1624 and began to put down roots in parts of the present-day states of New York, Delaware, Connecticut, and New Jersey. The Dutch struggled to maintain their colony. While they had established numerous social and economic relationships with local Lenape communities, they found it difficult to attract settlers to New Amsterdam, especially to southern regions of the colony

(Jacobs 2005:37–38). The growth of English settlements in neighboring New England and conflict between England and the Netherlands eventually led to the end of New Netherland. Governor Peter Stuyvesant was forced to surrender New Amsterdam, which was soon renamed New York, to an English fleet in 1664.

In the late nineteenth century, a small collection of objects from the Abbott Farm site in Trenton, New Jersey, found their way to the Peabody Museum in Cambridge, Massachusetts. Museum records indicate that these objects were excavated from the farmstead by Charles Conrad Abbott, an avocational archaeologist under the tutelage of Frederic Ward Putnam, director of the Peabody Museum. A label in the accession file, presumably written in the hand of Abbott, indicates that he excavated the material from the site of a 1668 "Dutch Trader's House" on the south end of Burlington Island, which is located in the Delaware River.

Burlington Island had been settled by two Dutch families and eight single men in the 1620s (Veit 2002:24). This small settlement was the locus of trading in the region until Alexander d'Hinoyossia, vice-director of New Netherland, moved his family to the island in the 1650s and added more structures to the small community (Veit 2002:25–26). It was likely one of the structures of this small community that Abbott excavated in the late nineteenth century.

Abbott recovered artifacts of adornment from the site that included 65 assorted glass beads, two copper tinkling cones, and two hematite pendants (Figures 5.2a, b, and c). Additionally, Abbott excavated porcelain (a French term for wampum), amber, and copper beads (PM accession file 52–46). Such an assemblage of adornment items would seem to indicate Native American-style dress: glass beads and tinkling cones could be attached to clothing, wampum beads were worn as belts or jewelry, and hematite pendants would be worn around the neck in a style that was closely aligned with the dress of the Lenape people living in the region. Lenape dress was most likely more complex than such an interpretation, however. Archaeological evidence from other sites in the region suggests that Lenape people often incorporated aspects of English and Dutch clothing and adornment into their fashions because of the ready availability of many kinds of cloth (Veit 2002:106–110). Abbott's excavation of other material from the site, including hundreds of white and red pipe fragments, wine bottles, iron nails, window glass, and clay roof tiles, led him, and later Veit and Bello

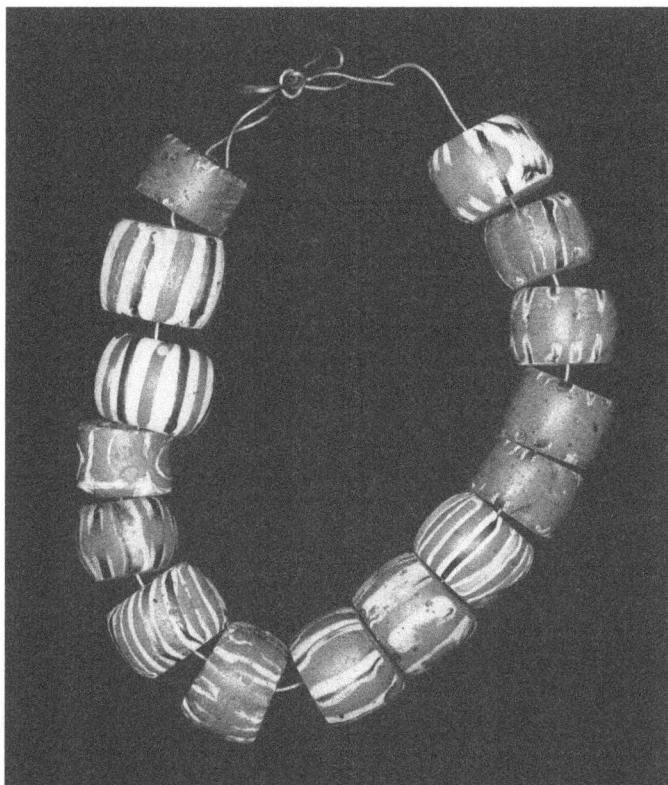

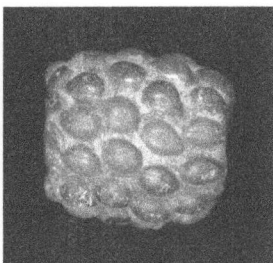

5.2a, b, and c. Artifacts of clothing and adornment recovered from the Abbott Site, Burlington Island, New Jersey. Courtesy of President and Fellows of Harvard College, Peabody Museum of Archaeology and Ethnology.

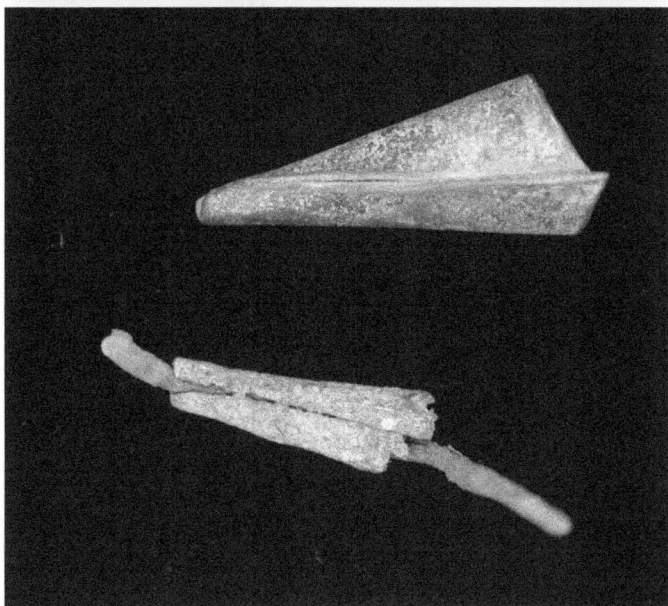

(1999:100, 110–115), to date the site to the mid-seventeenth century during the period of Dutch settlement.

In a recent analysis of this material, Veit and Bello (1999:98, 101–103) note that there was also a Lenape settlement on Burlington Island; the Lenape name for the island was Tinnagconc. In their discussion of the question of ethnicity in relation to these objects, Veit and Bello had trouble reconciling the items of Native American manufacture (the hematite pendants, copper beads, tinkling cones, and wampum) with European-manufactured arti-facts of adornment (glass beads) recovered from the site. They wondered whether the Dutch traders living at the site were curating Native American material.

Their analysis resonates with me, not only because of the question of ethnicity, but also because of their questioning of curatorial practice. Many who interpret early colonial-period European settlements assume that Eu-ropeans held on to Native American-manufactured objects only for the sake of curiosity (perhaps as a measure of racial and social difference) and not as objects to be used in their own daily activities. The underlying as-sumption of such interpretations is that Native American–made objects could not have meaning in the life of someone with a European worldview. A similar assumption exists for the European-manufactured "trade goods" found at the site. It is assumed that these items were part of Europeans' warehouse of trade goods rather than as items they could incorporate into their daily lives. When archeologists find European-manufactured items in Native American contexts (particularly glass beads in burials), they link their presence to notions of meaning. That is, researchers assume that Native peoples were eager to include the "exotic" into their worldviews. But why is this kind of interpretation so rarely forwarded when Native American-manufactured items (e.g., tinkling cones) are recovered from European contexts, especially since Native American-manufactured items are commonly recovered from colonial-period European sites in the New World?

Rothschild (2003:192) notes that the Dutch maintained a social distance from neighboring Native peoples (see also Baart 1987; Huey 1991). Dutch ministers made few attempts to Christianize local Native American popula-tions in New Netherland, and there was little sexual contact between Dutch male settlers and Native American women (Rothschild 1996:190). Of course there were deviations from this pattern. For example, Arent Van Curler, magistrate of Albany and one of the founders of Schenectady settlement, fathered a daughter in 1652 with a Mohawk woman (Bradley 2007:93). But sexual interactions did not necessarily result in the co-mingling of material culture. Although some Native American–manufactured artifacts were recovered from Dutch homesteads in New Amsterdam, there is no indication that the inhabitants used these objects (Rothschild 2003:194; 1996:193).

Paul Huey (1988:568–570) indicates that glass beads and wampum were the most frequent items of adornment recovered from excavations at Fort Orange (in present-day Albany, New York). In addition to these items of adornment, however, black glass and brass buttons, aglets, and hooks and eyes as well as Dutch lead fabric seals were also recovered from the site. Historical accounts suggest that the Dutch often obtained items of clothing from the English; the practice was so common that a Swedish visitor to Albany in the eighteenth century remarked that while the settlers spoke Dutch and had Dutch manners, "they dressed like the English" (Shannon 1996:21). In addition, while the primary form of interaction between Dutch and Native inhabitants of New Netherland was for the purposes of trade, Dutch settlers choose to trade only for furs and food, not for household items (Huey 1988:251; Rothschild 1996:189, 193). Based on this information, we assume that Dutch people living at the house on Burlington Island never wore the items of adornment that Abbott recovered. But unlike at Fort Orange, no other items of clothing and adornment were recovered from Abbott Farm, and here we are left to wonder if it is really the case that the recovered items were not added to the clothing and adornment strategies of Dutch people living on Burlington Island.

The pattern of Dutch colonialism sketched out by Huey, Rothschild, and Veit seems to indicate that the Dutch and Lenape people kept separate residences on Burlington Island. Peabody Museum records also indicate, however, that a Lenape woman was buried at the site. Her presence has not been factored in to interpretations of the site and the artifacts recovered there. It would be easy to say that the Native American material was the result of her presence there, but what was her relationship to the Dutch men or women living there? Was this site her own home? Why was this site not interpreted as multiethnic? The answers lie in long-standing tendency of researchers to base their interpretations of the ethnicity of individuals living at a particular site on the ways that archaeologists categorize material culture: that is, since the architectural style of the house was European, then the occupants must have been European as well. This classification scheme separates people and their activities into discreet units as either

"Native" or "European." But this categorization yields almost no information about the ways that individuals used material culture in processes of identity formation. Artifacts acquire symbolic meaning and value through use and activities rather than through categories that are assigned to them based on where they were produced, an interpretive bias that overlooks the possibility of multiethnic households (Jones 1997; Lightfoot 1995; Loren 2004, 2007a).

During the colonial period, mixed-blood, African, Native American, and European men and women of a variety of social and economic backgrounds created multiethnic communities throughout colonial America (e.g., Rothschild 1996, 2003; St. George 2000). So while Dutch and Native peoples often maintained separate residences in New Netherland, the context of Abbott Farm illustrates the permeability of those boundaries: a Lenape woman lived and was buried at the site, and a variety of Native American objects of adornment were recovered there. The community clearly was multiethnic and the lives of Dutch and Lenape people were intertwined—perhaps not sexually, but certainly economically and socially. These entanglements took form in daily life, including through practices of dress, where distinct cultural traditions met and reshaped social, sexual, and political interactions.

Clothed in French Louisiana: The Grand Village of the Natchez

Located along the east bank of the Mississippi River in what is now southwestern Mississippi, the Grand Village of the Natchez was occupied during the period 1682–1729 (Neitzel 1965). The Grand Village, a mound and village complex with a large central plaza, was the main ceremonial center for the tribe (Neitzel 1965). The Natchez had occupied this area of the American Southeast for several centuries before the French explored the region in the late seventeenth century (Neitzel 1965; Usner 1992).

In the early eighteenth century, the French established small households and plantations in the Natchez area; in 1729, they established Fort Rosalie there. As in many colonial situations, interactions between the French and the Natchez were fraught with violence, which culminated in the 1729 movement against the French now known as the Natchez Massacre, in which most of the French inhabitants of Fort Rosalie were killed. Ensuing violence between the French and the Natchez resulted in the dispersal of the Natchez from their homelands. Many Natchez refugees joined other tribes, including the Chickasaws, the Creeks, and the Cherokees. Today, people of Natchez descent live among the Creek and Cherokee Indians but without federal or state recognition as a Native American tribe (Barnett 2007; National Park Service 2008).

In Louisiana, it was believed that intermarriage with Native American women would foster alliances that would enable the French to survive in new terrain. Such alliances would also provide new souls ready for conversion, which was an explicit goal of French colonial projects (Hawthorne 1991; Rowland and Dunbar 1929:233; Spear 1999, 2003: 32). Through the work of Capuchin and Jesuit missionaries and some of the more pious settlers, Native peoples living in Louisiana learned about Christian notions of sin and promiscuity. Religious conversion was less than successful among the Natchez, however, as Father Gravier noted in 1708:"Monsieur de St. Cosme had not made a Single Christian among the Natche[z]" (Gravier 1708:129). Similarly, detailed descriptions written by French planter Le Page du Pratz on Natchez burial and ceremonial practices suggest that Natchez people never changed their religious and belief systems to follow Christian beliefs (Le Page du Pratz 1975).

This did not preclude numerous sexual relationships between Natchez women and French men living at Fort Rosalie (Dawdy 2006; Spear 1999, 2003:32). For example, French settler and author Antoine Simone Le Page du Pratz had a long-standing relationship with a Chitimatcha Indian woman. Like other French men in the colony, he had no problem with interracial sexual relations (Dawdy 2006:154). Did these intimate relationships as well as numerous economic, social, and diplomatic engagements between the French and the Natchez impact dress in Native American communities?

Historical images of the Natchez and many other Native peoples living in the Lower Mississippi Valley suggest otherwise; in these images Native peoples are depicted as altering their fashions only minimally. In 1734, Alexandre de Batz depicted Native American warriors wearing little else but cloth about their middle (Figure 5.3) Forty years later, Le Page du Pratz depicted a Natchez woman and her daughter in much the same way (Figure 5.4).

Colonial narratives provide a bit more information and texture to our understanding of how Natchez people changed their fashions. French authors were fascinated by the ways that Natchez peoples, especially women,

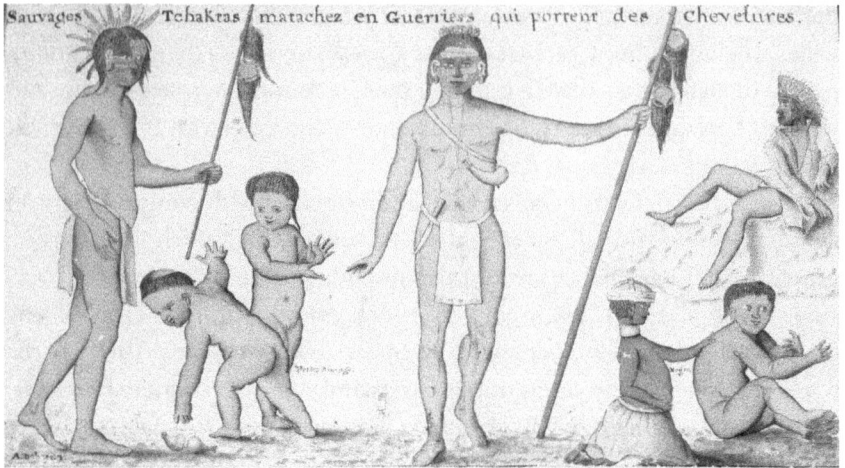

5.3. *Sauvages Tchaktas Matachez en Guerriers*, watercolor by Alexandre De Batz, ca. 1734. Courtesy of President and Fellows of Harvard College, Peabody Museum of Archaeology and Ethnology, 41-72-10/19.

adorned their bodies. For example, Le Page du Pratz (1975:137) described the dress of Natchez women as exotic:

From their belts to their knees hang many strings from the same cord [ribbon] which are attached claws of birds or prey like eagles, tiercelets, buzzards, etc., which when these girls walk make a kind of clicking, which pleases them.

Similarly, French engineer Dumont de Montigny noted that "their tresses are ordinarily laced by way of ornament with strings of blue, white, green, or black beads [made of glass]" (quoted in Swanton 1911:51). Du Pratz also described a warrior's dress:

All the attire of a warrior consists in the ear pendants, which I have just described, in a belt ornamented with rattles—and bells when they can get them from the French (quoted in Swanton 1911:127).

The account of Father Le Petit, a Jesuit missionary, complicates our understanding of Natchez dress, however. He noted in 1730 that among the captives the Natchez spared in the massacre were a tailor and French women who knew how to sew European clothing. He wrote, "The least miserable [captives] were those who knew how to sew, because they kept them busy making shirts, dresses, etc" (Le Petit 1730:165–167). Clearly, the static visual

5.4. "A Natchez woman and girl." From Le Page du Pratz,
The History of Louisiana (1774, 37).

images of resistance to European clothing styles that Alexandre de Batz and Le Page du Pratz offered were not completely accurate depictions of the reality of Natchez clothing styles in the eighteenth century; Natchez people wanted European-style clothing.

How does the archaeological record add to our understanding of the complexity of cultural exchange among Natchez peoples and French colonialists? Archaeological investigations at the Grand Village of the Natchez, also known as the Fatherland site, were conducted in 1930, 1962, and 1972. The most thorough studies on the site were published by Robert Neitzel (1965, 1983). Moreau Chambers excavated several burials from Mound C at the site in the 1930s, and Neitzel later published these excavations as part of the site report on his own excavations at the site in 1962 (Neitzel 1965:40–47). In the 1970s, Neitzel returned to the site to conduct excavations at several of the mounds and the large plaza area (Neitzel 1983).

Artifacts of clothing and adornment recovered from the Fatherland site's domestic and burial contexts include shell ear pins, brass and copper tinklers, brass thimbles, Jesuit rings, religious medals, one- and two-part coat buttons, brass bells, shoe and belt buckles, and thousands of glass beads (Neitzel 1965:48–51; 1983). This variety of European-manufactured and Native American–manufactured clothing and adornment items is not surprising. Overall, the material assemblage from the site shares similarities with assemblages from other colonial sites in the region in that Native American-manufactured material was often found in combination with European-manufactured items in domestic and burial contexts. These combinations of European-manufactured and Natchez-manufactured items indicate the extent to which Natchez peoples incorporated French material culture into their lives and daily practices.

A comparison of the visual and historical records with the archaeological material recovered from the Fatherland site lays bare the limitations of some historical sources. Visual representations produced by de Batz and Le Page du Pratz fail to capture the detail and complexity of dress practices; they provide only a simplified view of the ways that Natchez people dressed. They depict them in an idealized fashion wearing more "traditional" dress: naked apart from cloth about their middle and tattoos. Neither of these depictions shows Native peoples wearing European-manufactured clothing or adornment, which we know the Natchez desired from Le Petit's quote that they spared women and tailors in the Natchez massacre. Archaeological material challenges the accuracy of these sources, indicating that

Natchez people drew from a variety of different clothing and adornment choices available to them to construct new identities in the Lower Mississippi Valley.

The details of clothing and adornment assemblage are worth discussing here. One adult at the site (Burial 15) was buried wearing a woolen frock coat—a *justaucorps* much like those described at Fort Michlimackinac—as indicated by the recovery of a three-foot length of brass buttons, spanning the distance between the individual's neck and knees. Iron coils hung from the individual's ears, and white, blue, and black glass beads were recovered around the neck of the individual (Neitzel 1965:43). This is the only example of a Natchez individual clothed in a French-style coat at the Fatherland site. While individuals in other burials at the site were interred with various combinations of glass beads, tinkling cones, thimbles, buttons, bells, coils, religious medallions, and finger rings, no evidence remains to suggest that any other individual at the site was interred wearing an article of clothing.

Another example of a Native American individual buried wearing a frock coat is from the Bloodhound site, an eighteenth-century Tunica Indian community and cemetery located in present-day western Mississippi (Brain 1988:162–174). At the site, an adult female was buried wearing shell ear pins and a European frock coat with wide leather cuffs and large copper-covered wooden buttons. Several matching brass buttons found near the pelvis suggest that she was wearing trousers. Hundreds of small white glass beads found to the right of her head suggest that these beads were woven into her hair, a practice of hair adornment often described by eighteenth-century French authors (Brain 1988:170–171). In both of these examples, the fact that a Native American was wearing a European-made coat was an embodiment of changing identity: the coat was worn in combination with glass beads and other Native American items of adornment. The incorporation of French coats along with glass beads, rings, coils, and other items into the sartorial world of Natchez and Tunica people was strategic. It materialized power, creativity, and the ability of these peoples to incorporate both the familiar and unfamiliar in their world and on their bodies.

Another category of adornment artifacts that stands out is glass beads. Glass beads of all varieties were recovered in burial and nonburial contexts at the Grand Village (Neitzel 1965:51). The quantity and quality of beads from the site suggest that glass was an important medium for Natchez people. Historical accounts of Natchez uses of glass resonate here. For example,

Father Le Petit, the Jesuit missionary, discussed the extent to which the Natchez valued glass and placed it within their main temple building as an object of reverence (Swanton 1911:269). Moreover, eighteenth-century colonial authors seem to have been fixated by the ways that Natchez women wore glass beads around their body and in their hair in particularly lavish and sexual ways.

Glass beads found in nonburial contexts at the Grand Village include a wide variety of drawn tubular and wire-wound glass beads similar to those commonly found at mid-eighteenth century sites in the colonial Southeast. These included medium-sized blue, white, and green glass beads; polychrome beads; dark amber to black flattened spherical beads; porcelain beads; medium-red opaque, drawn, tubular white, and blue glass beads; and raspberry beads (Neitzel 1965:51; 1983:109–110). These beads were found in proximity to other items of clothing and adornment recovered from nonburial contexts: shoe buckles, buttons, tinkling cones, and iron coil earrings (Neitzel 1983:111–114).

In contrast to beads found in nonburial contexts, the majority of glass beads recovered from burials are medium-sized blue or white beads worn as necklaces. Shell beads and in fact shell artifacts in general—with the exception of one shell ear pin—are absent from the site. This absence is striking in this context as glass beads are often found in combination with shell beads in Native American sites in the colonial Eastern Woodlands. Additionally, there is little archaeological or historical evidence to suggest that Natchez people wore or made beaded clothing. Rather, their investment of labor related to beads was limited to stringing them into necklaces of distinct color combinations. In almost every instance, they wore glass beads in combination with both Native American– and European-manufactured material, suggesting the importance of glass beads in the lived experiences of Natchez peoples.

Glass beads were the materialization of the Natchez people's intimate and economic relations with the French that had reshaped their community and sense of self. While there is no information about why the color blue was so important to the Natchez we do know that they frequently located blue beads close to the face in burial contexts. It is no coincidence that glass beads were the items that were chosen so frequently among other kinds of European-manufactured items, including other items of clothing and adornment. The properties of glass—color, sound, and translucence— were meaningful to the Natchez in the context of the ways they adorned

5.5. "A Chief Lady of Pomeiooc, by Theodor de Bry after John White." Plate 8 from Theodor de Bry, *America*, Part 1, 1590.

their bodies; they were placed with loved ones at the time of death, worn near the face as necklaces, and woven into hair. Turgeon (2004, 2006) argues that in many Native American communities, beads carried notions of protection and spiritual well-being in an afterlife; perhaps the same was true for the Natchez. The primacy of beads in the archaeological assemblage suggests beads were more than just simple adornment for the Natchez people. Rather, they used them to physically embody new understandings of self and the body that they created through their associations with the French.

Lindman and Tarter (2001:2) argue that "bodies are maps for reading the past through lived experience, metaphorical expression, and precepts of representation." They place the body at the center of studies of the colonial world, where "many bodies and many interpretations of bodies were coming together in a transitional world of cultural contact, conquest, adaptation in early America" (Lindman and Tarter 2001:5; see also Loren 2007a). In this context, the measurement and classification of difference was intimately tied to the body and bodily presentation (Stoler 1997). Images such as the illustration by Theodor de Bry (after John White) in Figure 5.5 indicate such colonial concerns.

John White illustrated an Algonquian woman and her daughter wearing beads around their necks. The woman is tattooed and wears a deerskin about her waist. Her daughter is naked with the exception of a covering over her privates, but in her hand she holds a doll clothed in Elizabethan dress. The text accompanying this image reads, "They [girls] are greatly delighted with puppets, and babies [dolls] which were brought out of England." The subtext that underlies this image is that White, de Bry, and Hariot all believed that if properly guided and schooled, Native peoples could become civilized; that they could make themselves into the image of the English. Not an exact replica, of course, but a properly clothed and adorned facsimile.

Such imaginings of progress and sartorial order had little basis in reality in colonial America. The body is where engagements were lived, felt, experienced, and understood by every actor in the colonial world. In the context of these engagements, clothing and adornment were aspects of self that were open to negotiation and reinterpretation. Doing these tasks through dress was just one strategy European peoples and Native peoples used to understood self and other in this changing world; a process by which people from different backgrounds became "colonial" in early America (St. George 2000).

6

~ ❀ ~

Conclusions and a Backward Glance

It was always an event in the little girl's life to take a walk with her father, and more particularly so today, because she had on her new winter bonnet, which was so beautiful (and so becoming) that for the first time she woke to the importance of dress, and of herself as a subject for adornment—so that I may date from that hour the birth of the conscious and feminine ME in the little girl's vague soul.
—Edith Wharton, *A Backward Glance*

In this book I have provided just a few examples of how colonial individuals in North America manipulated clothing and adornment in their embodiment of self. While these colonial contexts differ quite a bit, they each raise several significant points: first, it was common for people to actively manipulate items of clothing and adornment within colonial contexts; and second, individuals manipulated seemingly mundane items in ways that were meaningful to them. They constituted their identities by producing, exchanging, and using things—that is, in the entanglement of subject and object (Gosden and Knowles 2001:5). The strategies people used in dressing were a way to build identity from the skin outward. Such actions were purposeful, suggesting that hybridity of dress was part of the strategy from the outset of colonial encounters and that creating hybrid fashion was a common colonial experience, shared by people of different ethnic and racial descent living in the American colonies.

The topic of clothing and adornment has been revitalized within historical archaeology by the growth in the literature that examines how sexuality, gender, materiality, and identity are situated on and in the body. Objects are at the center of research related to clothing and adornment: people embodied identity through their use of objects on their bodies. Colonial peoples did not simply hang objects on their bodies to clothe nakedness;

such actions were purposeful. They embodied their identities through their use of material culture. The objects of clothing and adornment they wore became part of their bodies and were integral to how they constructed their identities for themselves and for others. And because practices of dress through clothing and adornment were so important, they were strictly monitored during the colonial period of North America. Social stigmas, fines, floggings, and even imprisonment were among the punishments meted out for dressing outside of prescribed fashions. Some individuals were forced to dress in a certain way; others carried the physical mark of their body's ownership by another.

In my discussions of the different strategies people used to dress their bodies, I do not mean to imply that they manipulated dress in every possible instance. Fashion occurred largely in public, where people created dress and identity with certain types of sumptuous and plain material culture. In some cases, they used clothing and adornment in nuanced and conservative ways as they constructed their identities. Barbara Voss argues that people at El Presidio de San Francisco used moderate manipulations of dress and adornment, for example (Voss 2008a:252–286; see also Voss 2008b). As she explains, colonial men and women were well aware of colonial sumptuary laws and what it meant to dress properly both at home and in church. At El Presidio de San Francisco, the archaeological record indicates that variation of dress occurred within a very narrow range. Everyday dress for the Californios was plain and their adornment, such as dark gray glass beads, was minimal (Voss 2008b:283). Attending religious services provided the population with an opportunity to dress up, to display wealth and status in more overt ways. Silks and lace did circulate through the community, but the archaeological record from the site indicates that the overall the dress of people at the presidio, regardless of race or status, was modest and did not fully follow the Bourbon fashion that was popular in other parts of New Spain (Voss 2008b:285; see also Loren 2007b for a discussion of dress in eastern New Spain). In addition, the population at El Presidio de San Francisco chose not to incorporate Native California dress styles, such as bone and shell beads and pendants, into their emerging fashions. The modest dress styles of presidio inhabitants and their disinclination to incorporate Native Californian dress into their clothing habits suggests a certain pattern of colonial life regarding the choices people made to create their emergent Californio identities. As Voss (2008b:286) concludes, Californio identity "was achieved as much through emphatic distinction from Native

Californians as it was through challenges to the arbitrary racial hierarchies that permeated the Spanish-colonial Americas."

Following the American Revolution, standards of dress changed rapidly: from combinations of homespun and imported clothing to the European fashions that influenced the emerging nation so deeply (De Marly 1990:131; Ulrich 2001). Although sumptuary laws were no longer being strictly enforced, dress continued to be monitored and judged as an important aspect of class and identity. Thomas Jefferson expressed as much in a letter to his 11-year-old daughter Martha:

> To advise you on the subject of dress, which I know you are a little apt to neglect. I do not wish you to be gaily clothed at this time of life, but that what you wear should be fine of its kind. But above all things and at all times, let your clothes be neat, whole, and properly put on. Do not fancy you must wear them till the dirt is visible to the eye. . . . Some ladies think they may, under the privileges of *déshabillée*, be loose and negligent of their dress in the morning. But be you from the moment you rise till you go to bed, as cleanly and properly dressed as at the hours of dinner or tea. A lady who is seen as a sloven or a slut in the morning, will never efface the impression she has made, with all the dress and pageantry she can afterwards involve herself in. (quoted in De Marly 1990:137–138)

As America as a concept and as a country grew during the nineteenth century, concerns about clothing and adornment continued but in a slightly different vein. Certain items of clothing and objects of adornment were increasingly mass-produced and distributed to peoples across social classes. Renegotiations of dress and identity were intertwined with the social identities of newly freed African peoples and Native Americans who were subject to federal Indian policies that promoted assimilation during the mid- to late nineteenth century.

One of the most striking examples of the manipulation of dress in a postcolonial context took place in the context of the Indian boarding schools of the nineteenth and twentieth centuries. In 1878, Captain Richard Pratt opened the Carlisle Indian School in Carlisle, Pennsylvania. Between 1880 and 1902, approximately 100 boarding schools were built off reservations to school approximately 30,000 Native American children and force them to assimilate into mainstream white culture (Archuleta et al. 2000; De Cunzo 2006:181).

6.1. Omaha Girls at Carlisle Indian School, ca. 1900. From left: Lettie Esan, Mary Hewett, Elsie Springer, Mary Lyndall, Alice Springer, Etta Webster, Jenny Mitchell, Fanny Mervice, Alice Tremont, Etta Lyndall, and Mamie Springer. Courtesy of President and Fellows of Harvard College, Peabody Museum of Archaeology and Ethnology, 2004.29.5870.

The goal of Indian boarding schools was to remove Native American children from home communities and place them in military-style institutions where traditional ways were replaced by Christian religion, household skills, and industrial trades. To achieve these goals, Native American children were subject to severe bodily changes: they were prohibited from speaking Native American languages, their hair was cut, and they were dressed in uniforms (Figure 6.1). Such alterations had immediate and traumatic impacts on how these children presented and experienced their selves.

The United States Industrial Indian School at Phoenix, Arizona, was one of these institutions where over 900 students from 23 tribes in Arizona, New Mexico, California, Nevada, and Oregon were schooled during the period 1891 to 1905 (De Cunzo 2006:181; Lindauer 1997:1–3). Artifacts recovered from a sanitary landfill that dates to the period 1892–1924 suggest how the students at the Phoenix Indian school developed strategies for incorporating their Native American identities with newly enforced American identities (Lindauer 1996, 1997:46–56). While the landfill provides evidence of the clothing school authorities used to impose conformity and military discipline on the students (brass buttons from uniforms and glass buttons from shirts, dresses, and undergarments), it also provides evidence of the ways that students strove to secretly retain other aspects of Native American identities through concealing and carrying fetishes and effigies on their bodies (Lindauer 1997:18–49; see also Casella 2007). While very little archaeology has been conducted at other Indian boarding schools, one hopes that future archaeologists will be able to investigate these contested institutions to recover similar corporeal and dressing strategies to those found at the Phoenix Indian School, practices Native American children enacted to diminish feelings of isolation from their home communities and identities.

Dress Matters

Dress is a discursive daily practice of constructing and reconstructing one's identity in a social landscape. Dress occurs at the micro level: colonial-era individuals constituted identity through material culture in relationship to sumptuary laws, imperial definitions of inclusion and exclusion, and lived experiences in colonial worlds (Fisher and Loren 2003). The archaeological record is a key component of interpreting the colonial past because all colonial relations were constituted with material culture (Gosden and Knowles 2001:6).

The work of understanding the clothed, adorned body within the colonial world relies heavily on the use of multiple sources. Material culture and textual and visual sources provide distinct, often contradictory, viewpoints about the nature of dress—how fashion, style, and meaning were embodied. One of the great advantages of interdisciplinary endeavors is that silences and disjunctures between sources can illuminate points of contention about colonial policy and practice (Hall 1992, 2000; Loren and Baram 2007; Stahl 1993). What can we learn of the lives and struggles of colonial peoples from investigating artifact assemblages that at first glance seem to contain unlikely and dissonant combinations of different categories of material culture? The answer lies in comparing artifacts that are present in the assemblage and in comparing the artifacts that have been retrieved with those that are missing, taking note of ways that the remnants of daily practices are or are not represented in historical, visual, and ethnographic material.

As a museum professional, I cannot help but reflect on the concerns related to displaying and interpreting clothing and adornment in colonial America. Archaeologists and historians now strive to tell a story in U.S. museums that incorporates all peoples and all experiences. A more inclusive picture of the people of colonial America has emerged through interpretations of material objects, which in the past were often interpreted through the lens of Western ideologies rather than the histories of people from many ethnic and racial groups (see Berlo and Phillips 1992; Smith and Wobst 2005). But spaces that seek to incorporate all viewpoints are in short supply, and as stewards of this past we have a responsibility to bring this multivocal history to the general public. Working with descendant communities has revitalized museum collections, allowing us to more fully understand the ways that people in North America purposefully and creatively constructed their distinct and meaningful identities through clothing and adornment. Some of these interactions were brought about through NAGPRA, and over time these conversations have evolved beyond NAGPRA into public areas in the museum.

Critical self-reflection on the practice of archaeology has brought about significant changes in the academic study of how people and objects intersected in their practices of clothing and adornment. Scholars are now interested in embodied practices rather than in a discussion of object divorced from body. In this book, I have argued for an approach to material culture that speaks to the intersections of body and objects that more aptly characterizes the identities that people constructed as they clothed and adorned their bodies.

In my own backward glance, I remember aspects of my life through the clothing and adornment I have embodied: those terrible corrective shoes made by my maternal grandfather, a crisp emerald prom dress, the scapular my mother would pin to my blouse before an important test, and the black clothes I have worn in mourning. My dress has continued to change as my identities have formed over time: student, glassblower, archaeologist, curator, and mother. The clothing and adornments that enclosed my skin as part of these identities were and are transformative.

This inward gaze suggests how we might come to view the lived experience of the clothed body in the world through the bits and fragments we recover in the archaeological record along with visual, historical, and ethnographic materials. As I hope the discussions in this book have indicated, an archaeological understanding of the clothed, adorned colonial body, the ways that individuals embodied self with material culture, is within our reach. Through archaeology we can begin to understand the complex entanglements of subject and object, of bodies and clothing, allowing us to get beyond the single glass bead to the experience of the person within the clothed, adorned body, living his or her life in colonial America.

References Cited

Adams, Diane L.

1989　*Lead Seals from Fort Michilimackinac, 1715–1781*. Archaeological Completion Report Series, No. 14. Mackinac State Historic Parks, Mackinac Island, Michigan.

African Burial Ground, National Park Service

2008　The African Burial Ground: Return to the Past to Build the Future. Electronic document, http://www.africanburialground.gov/ABG_Main.htm, accessed September 2, 2008.

Anderson, Dean

1991　Variability in Trade at Eighteenth-Century French Outposts. In *French Colonial Archaeology: The Illinois County and the Western Great Lakes*, edited by John A. Walthall, pp. 218–236. University of Illinois Press, Urbana.

1994　The Flow of European Trade Goods into the Western Great Lakes Region, 1715–1760. In *The Fur Trade Revisited*, edited by J. S. H. Brown, W. J. Eccles and D.P. Heldman, pp. 93–115. Michigan State University Press, East Lansing and Mackinac State Historic Parks, Mackinac Island.

Anderson, Fiona

2005　Fashion: Style, Identity, and Meaning. In *Exploring Visual Culture: Definitions, Concepts, Contexts,* edited by M. Rampley, pp. 67–84. Edinburgh University Press, Edinburgh.

Archuleta, Margaret, Brenda J. Child, and K. Tsianina Lomawaima

2000　*Away from Home: American Indian Boarding School Experiences, 1879–2000.* Museum of New Mexico Press, Albuquerque.

Aultman, Jennifer, and Kate Grillo

2003　DAACS Cataloging Manual: Buttons. Digital Archaeological Archive of Chesapeake Slavery. Electronic document, www.daacs.org, accessed February 8, 2008.

Avery, George

1995 More friend than foe: Eighteenth-century Spanish, French, and Caddoan interaction at Los Adaes, a capital of Texas located in northwestern Louisiana. *Louisiana Archaeology* 22: 163–193.

Baart, Jan M.

1987 Dutch Material Civilization: Daily Life between 1650–1776, Evidence from Archaeology. In *New World Dutch Studies: Dutch Arts and Culture in Colonial America, 1609–1776*, edited by Roderic H. Blackburn and Nancy A. Kelley, pp. 1–12. Albany Institute of History and Art, Albany, New York.

Bach, Rebecca Ann

2000 *Colonial Transformations: The Cultural Production of the New Atlantic World, 1580–1640*. Macmillan, New York.

Baram, Uzi

2007 Images of the Holy Land: The David Roberts Paintings as Artifacts of 1830s Palestine. *Historical Archaeology* 41(1):106–117.

Barber, Russell J.

1984 Treasures in the Peabody's Basement. *Bulletin of the Massachusetts Archaeological Society* 45(2):49–51.

Barnett, Jim

2007 Mississippi History Now: The Natchez Indians. Electronic document, http://mshistory.k12.ms.us/index.php?id=4, accessed June 5, 2008.

Barnes, Ruth, and Joanne B. Eicher

1993 *Dress and Gender: Making and Meaning in Cultural Contexts*. Berg, Oxford.

Baumgarten, Linda

2002 *What Clothes Reveal: The Language of Clothing in Colonial and Federal America*. Colonial Williamsburg Foundation in association with Yale University Press, Williamsburg, Virginia.

Beaudry, Mary C.

1988 *Documentary Archaeology in the New World*. Cambridge University Press, Cambridge.

2006 *Findings: The Material Culture of Needlework and Sewing*. Yale University Press, New Haven, Connecticut.

Berlo, Janet C., and Ruth C. Phillips

1998 *Native North American Art*. Oxford Press, Oxford.

Bianchi, Leonard G., and Barbara A. Bianco

2006 Buttons and Fasteners. In *New York African Burial Ground Archaeology Final Report*, Vol. 1, edited by Warren R. Perry, Jean Howson and Barbara A. Bianco, pp. 306–381. Also available as an electronic document, http://www.africanburialground.gov/FinalReports/Archaeology/ABG_Ch12FEB.pdf, accessed September 23, 2008.

Bollwerk, Elizabeth

2006   Controlling Acculturation: A Potawatomi Strategy for Avoiding Removal. *Midcontinental Journal of Archaeology* 31(1):117–142.

Bourdieu, Pierre

1984   *Distinction: A Social Critique of the Judgment of Taste.* Translated by William Nice. Harvard University Press, Cambridge, Massachusetts.

Bradley, James W.

2007   *Before Albany: An Archaeology of Native-Dutch Relations in the Capital Region, 1600–1664.* New York State Museum, Albany.

Brain, Jeffrey P.

1988   *Tunica Archaeology.* Peabody Museum of Archaeology and Ethnology, Harvard University, Cambridge, Massachusetts.

Brandão, José António, and Michael Shakir Nassaney

2008   Suffering for Jesus: Penitential Practices at Fort St. Joseph (Niles, MI) during the French Regime. *Catholic Historical Review* 94(3):476–499.

Brain, Jeffrey P.

1988   *Tunica Archaeology.* Papers of the Peabody Museum of Archaeology and Ethnography, vol. 78. Harvard University Press, Cambridge, Masssachusetts.

Breen, Thomas H.

1993   "Baubles of Britain": The American and Consumer Revolutions of the Eighteenth Century. In *Diversity and Unity in Early North America,* edited by Philip D. Morgan, pp. 161–182. Routledge, Oxford.

Butler, Judith

1990   *Gender Trouble: Feminism and the Subversion of Identity.* Routledge, London.

Burton, John W.

2001   *Culture and the Human Body: An Anthropological Perspective.* Waveland Press, Long Grove, Illinois.

Calefato, Patrizia

2004   *The Clothed Body.* Berg Publishers, Oxford.

Cannadine, David

2001   *Ornamentalism: How the British Saw Their Empire.* Oxford University Press, Oxford.

Caplan, Jane (editor)

2000   *Written on the Body: the Tattoo in European and American History.* Vintage Press, New York.

Capone, Patricia, and Diana D. Loren

2004   Stewardship of Sensitive Collections: Policies, Procedures, and Process of Their Development at the Peabody Museum. In *Stewards of the Sacred,* edited by Lawrence E. Sullivan and Alison Edwards. American Association of Museums Press, Washington, D.C.

Carrera, Magali Marie

2003 *Imagining Identity in New Spain: Race, Lineage, and the Colonial Body in Portraiture and Casta Paintings.* University of Texas Press, Austin.

Casella, Eleanor C.

2007 *The Archaeology of Institutional Confinement.* University Press of Florida, Gainesville.

Castelló Yturbide, Teresa

1990 La indumentaria de las castas del mestizaje. *Artes de México* 8:73–78.

Chan, Alexandra A.

2007 *Slavery in the Age of Reason: Archaeology at a New England Farm.* University of Tennessee Press, Knoxville.

Chaplin, Joyce E.

1997 Natural Philosophy and an Early Racial Idiom in North America: Comparing English and Indian Bodies. *William and Mary Quarterly* 54(1):229–252.

2003 *Subject Matter: Technology, the Body, and Science on the Anglo-American Frontier, 1500–1676.* Harvard University Press, Cambridge, Massachusetts.

Claasen, Cheryl

1994 Washboards, Pigtoes, and Muckets: Historical Musselling in the Mississippi Watershed. *Historical Archaeology* 28(2):1–138.

Colchester, Chlöe (editor)

2003 *Clothing the Pacific.* Berg Publishers, Oxford.

Colwell-Chanthaphonh, Chip, and T. J. Ferguson (editors)

2007 *Collaboration in Archaeological Practice: Engaging Descendant Communities.* Rowman and Littlefield, Lanham, Maryland.

Colonial Society of Massachusetts

1935 *Harvard College Records.* Part III. Boston: The Colonial Society of Massachusetts.

Comaroff, Jean

1996 The Empire's Old Clothes: Fashioning the Colonial Subject. In *Cross-Cultural Consumption: Global Markets, Local Realities,* edited by David Howes, pp. 19–38. Routledge Press, London.

Davidson, James M.

2004 Rituals Captures in Context and Time: Charm Use in North Dallas Freedman's Town (1869–1907), Dallas, Texas. *Historical Archaeology* 38(2):22–54.

Davis, Fred

1994 *Fashion, Culture, and Identity.* University of Chicago Press, Chicago.

Dawdy, Shannon Lee

2006 Proper Caresses and Prudent Distance: A How-To Manual from Colonial Louisiana. In *Haunted by Empire: Geographies of Intimacy in North Ameri-*

can History, edited by Ann Laura Stoler, pp. 140–162. Duke University Press, Durham, North Carolina.

Deagan, Kathleen A.

1988   Neither History or Prehistory: The Questions That Count in Historical Archaeology. *Historical Archaeology* 22(1):7–12

2002   *Artifacts of the Spanish Colonies of Florida and the Caribbean, 1500–1800,* Vol. 2. *Personal Portable Possessions.* Smithsonian Institution Press, Washington, D.C.

DeCunzo, Lu Ann

2006   Exploring the Institution: Reform, Confinement, and Social Change. In *Historical Archaeology,* edited by Stephen W. Silliman and Martin Hall, pp. 167–198. Blackwell Press, Oxford.

Degler, Carl N.

1984   *Out of Our Past: The Forces That Shaped Modern America.* Harper Collins, New York.

Deloria, Vine, Jr.

1988   *Custer Died for Your Sins: An Indian Manifesto.* University of Oklahoma Press, Norman.

De Marly, Diana

1990   *Dress in North America: The New World, 1492–1800.* Holmes and Meier, New York.

DeMarrais, Elizabeth, Chris Gosden, and Colin Renfrew

2004   *Rethinking Materiality: The Engagement of the Mind with the Material World.* Oxbow Books, London.

De Moraes Farias, Paulo Fernando

1985   Models of the World and Categorical Models: The "Enslavable Barbarian" as a Mobile Classificatory Label. In *Slaves and Slavery in Muslim Africa,* Vol. 1. *Islam and the Ideology of Enslavement,* edited by J. R. Willis Frank, pp. 27–45. Cass Press, London.

Egan, Geoff, with contributions by Mike Cowell and Hero Granger Taylor

1995   *Lead Cloth Seals and Related Items in the British Museum.* British Museum Occasional Papers #93. Department of Medieval and Later Antiquities. British Museum Press, London.

Eicher, Joanne B.

1999   *Dress and Ethnicity: Change across Space and Time.* Berg Publishers, Oxford.

Eicher, Joanne B., and Mary Ellen Roach-Higgins

1992   Definition and Classification of Dress: Implications for Analysis of Gender Roles. In *Dress and Gender: Making and Meaning,* edited by Ruth Barnes and Joanne B. Eicher, pp. 9–28. Berg Press, Oxford.

Ellis, Christopher J., and Neal Ferris

1990   *The Archaeology of Southern Ontario to* A.D. *1650.* Ontario Archaeological Society, London Chapter, London, Ontario.

Emery, Irene, and Patricia L. Fiske

1975   *Archaeological Textiles.* Textile Museum, Washington, D.C.

Entwistle, Joanne

2000   *The Fashioned Body: Fashion, Dress, and Modern Social Theory.* Polity Press, Cambridge.

Entwistle, Joanne, and Elizabeth Wilson

2001   Introduction: Body Dressing. In *Body Dressing,* edited by Joanne Entwistle and Elizabeth Wilson, pp. 1–9. Berg Publishers, Oxford.

Fisher, Genevieve and Diana DiPaolo Loren

2003   Embodying Identity in Anthropology and Archaeology. *Cambridge Archaeological Journal* 13(2):225–230.

Fitzgerald, William R.

1982   A Refinement of Historic Neutral Chronologies: Evidence from Shaver Hill, Christianson and Dwyer. *Ontario Archaeology* 38:31–46.

Francis, Peter, Jr.

1988   *Glass Trade Beads of Europe.* Lapis Route Books, Lake Placid.

Galle, Jillian E.

2005   Designing Women: Measuring Acquisition and Access at the Hermitage Plantation. In *Engendering African American Archaeology,* edited by Jillian E. Galle and Amy L. Young, pp. 39–72. University of Tennessee Press, Knoxville.

Gallivan, Martin D.

2003   *James River Chiefdoms: The Rise of Social Inequality in the Chesapeake.* University of Nebraska Press, Lincoln.

2004   Reconnecting the Contact Period and Late Prehistory: Household and Community Dynamics in the James River Basin. In *Indian and European Contact in Context: The Mid-Atlantic Region,* edited by Dennis B. Blanton and Julia A. King, pp. 22–46. University of Florida Press, Gainesville.

Gallivan, Martin D., Thane Harpole, David A. Brown, Danielle Moretti-Langholtz, and E. Randolph Turner, III

2006   *The Werowocomoco (44GL32) Research Project: Background and 2003 Archaeological Field Season Results.* Archaeological Research Report Series, No. 1, College of William & Mary, Department of Anthropology, Williamsburg, Virginia. Electronic document, http://powhatan.wm.edu/resources/downloads.htm, accessed November 21, 2008.

Galloway, Patricia K.

1991   The Archaeology of the Ethnohistorical Narrative. In *Colombian Conse-*

quences, Vol. 3. *The Spanish Borderlands in Pan-American Perspective,* edited by D. H. Thomas, pp. 453–469. Smithsonian Institution Press, Washington, D.C.

Goodwin, Lorinda B. R.

1999   *An Archaeology of Manners: The Polite World of the Merchant Elite of Colonial Massachusetts.* Springer Press, New York.

Gosden, Chris, and Chantal Knowles

2001   *Collecting Colonialism: Material Culture and Colonial Change.* Berg, Oxford.

Gravier, Father Jacques

1708   Letter of Father Jacques Gravier upon the Affairs of Louisiana. Letter dated February 23, 1708. In *The Jesuit Relations and Allied Documents,* Vol. 66, edited by Reuben Gold Thwaites, pp. 124–143. Pageant Book Co., New York.

Greenblatt, Stephen

1984   *Renaissance Self-Fashioning: From More to Shakespeare.* University of Chicago Press, Chicago.

Gregory, Hiram F. (editor)

1984   *Excavations 1981–82, Presidio de Nuestra Señora del Pilar de los Adaes.* Williamson Museum, Northwestern State University, Natchitoches, Louisiana.

Gregory, Hiram F., George Avery, Aubra L. Lee, and Jay C. Blaine

2004   Presidio Los Adaes: Spanish, French, and Caddoan Interaction on the Northern Frontier. *Historical Archaeology* 38(3):65–77.

Gregory, Hiram F. Gregory, George Avery, Francis X. Galán, Steve Black, Mariah Wade, Jay C. Blaine, and Aubra L. Lee

2009   Los Adaes: 18th-Century Capital of Spanish Texas. Electronic document, http://www.texasbeyondhistory.net/adaes/index.html, accessed January 8, 2010.

Hackett, Charles Wilson

1934   *Pichardo's Treatise on the Limits of Louisiana and Texas.* 5 vols. University of Texas Press, Austin.

Hall, Martin

1992   Small Things and the Mobile, Conflictual Fusion of Power, Fear, and Desire. In *The Art and Mystery of Historical Archaeology: Essays in Honor of James Deetz,* edited by Ann Yentsch and Mary Beaudry, pp. 373–399. CRC Press, Boca Raton, Florida.

2000   *Archaeology and the Modern World: Colonial Transcripts in South Africa and the Chesapeake.* Routledge Press, London and New York.

Hamell, George R.

1983   Trading and Metaphors: The Magic of Beads. In *Proceedings of the 1982 Glass Trade Bead Conference,* edited by Charles F. Hayes, III, pp. 5–28. Research

Record No. 16. Research Division, Rochester Museum and Science Center, Rochester, New York.

Hansen, Karen T.

2003　The World in Dress: Anthropological Perspectives on Clothing, Fashion, and Culture. *Annual Review of Anthropology* 33:369–92.

Hariot, Thomas

1590　*A Briefe and True Report of the New Found Land of Virginia,* illustrated by John White. Francoforti ad Moenum: Typis Ioannis Wecheli, sumtibus vero Theodri de Bry.

Hawthorne, Margaret

1991　"That Certain Piece of Furniture": Women in Colonial Louisiana, 1685–1763. *Journal of Mississippi History* 53(3):219–227.

Henrickson, Steve

2008　Tlingit Warriors and Their Armor. In *Anóoshi Lingit Aaní Ká: The Battles of Sitka, 1802 and 1804,* edited by Richard Dauenhauer and Lydia Black, pp. 389–394. University of Washington Press, Seattle.

Hill, Jude

2007　The Story of the Amulet: Locating the Enchantment of Collections. *Journal of Material Culture* 12(1):65–87.

Hinks, Stephen

1988　*A Structural and Functional Analysis of 18th Century Buttons.* Master's thesis, Department of Anthropology, The College of William and Mary, Williamsburg, Virginia.

Hodder, Ian

1990　Style as Historical Quality. In *The Uses of Style in Archaeology,* edited by Meg Conkey and Christine Hastorf, pp. 44–51. Cambridge University Press, Cambridge, Massachusetts.

Hollander, Anne

1993　*Seeing through Clothes.* University of California Press, Berkeley.

Huey, Paul R.

1988　*Aspects of Continuity and Change in Colonial Dutch Material Culture at Fort Orange, 1624–1664.* Ph.D. dissertation, University of Pennsylvania, Philadelphia.

1991　The Dutch at Fort Orange. In *Historical Archaeology in Global Perspective,* edited by Lisa Falk, pp. 21–67. Smithsonian Institution Press, Washington, D.C.

Hurlock, Elizabeth Bergner

1984　*The Psychology of Dress: An Analysis of Fashion and Its Motive.* Ayer Publishing, New York.

Jackson, Louise M.

1994　Cloth, Clothing, and Related Paraphernalia: A Key to Gender Visibility in the Archaeological Record of Russian America. In *Those of Little Note: Gender, Race, and Class in Historical Archaeology,* edited by Elizabeth M. Scott, pp. 27–54. University of Arizona Press, Tucson.

Jacobs, Jaap

2005　*New Netherland: A Dutch Colony in Seventeenth-Century America.* Brill, Boston.

Jones, Siân

1997　*The Archaeology of Ethnicity: Constructing Identities in the Past and the Present.* London: Routledge.

Joyce, Rosemary

1998　Performing the Body in Pre-Hispanic Central America. *RES: Anthropology and Aesthetics* 33:147–165.

2005　Archaeology of the Body. *Annual Review of Anthropology* 34: 139–158.

Karklins, Karlis

1985　*Glass Beads: The Nineteenth-Century Levin Catalogue and Venetian Bead Book and Guide to Description of Glass Beads.* Studies in Archaeology, Architecture, and History. Environment Parks Canada, Ottawa, Canada.

1992　*Trade Ornament Usage among the Native Peoples of Canada: A Source Book.* Minister of the Environment, Ottawa, Canada.

Katzew, Ilona

2004　*Casta Painting Images of Race in Eighteenth-Century Mexico: Images of Race in Eighteenth-Century Mexico.* Yale University Press, New Haven, Connecticut.

Kelso, William M., Nicholas M. Luccketti, and Beverly A. Straube

1997　*Jamestown Rediscovery III.* The Association for the Preservation of Virginia Antiquities, Richmond.

1999　*Jamestown Rediscovery V.* The Association for the Preservation of Virginia Antiquities, Richmond.

Kelso, William M., and Beverly A. Straube

2000　*Jamestown Rediscovery VI.* The Association for the Preservation of Virginia Antiquities, Richmond.

Kent, Barry C.

1983　The Susquehanna Bead Sequence. *Proceedings of the 1982 Glass Bead Conference,* edited by Charles F. Hayes, pp. 75–81, Research Records No. 16, Rochester Museum and Science Division, Rochester, New York.

Kent, Timothy J.

2001　*Ft. Pontchartrain at Detroit: A Guide to the Daily Lives of Fur Trade and Military Personnel, Settlers, and Missionaries at French Posts.* Wayne State University Press, Detroit, Michigan.

Kenyon, Ian T.

1982   *The Grimsby Site: A Historic Neutral Cemetery.* Royal Ontario Museum, Toronto.

Kidd, Kenneth A., and Martha A. Kidd

1970   A Classification System for Glass Beads for the Use of Field Archaeologists. *Canadian Historic Sites: Occasional Papers in Archaeology and History* 1:45–89.

King, Julia A.

2007   Still Life with Tobacco: The Archaeological Uses of Dutch Art. *Historical Archaeology* 41(1):6–22.

Kirch, Patrick V.

1997   *Feathered Gods and Fishhooks: An Introduction to Hawaiian Archaeology and Prehistory.* University of Hawaii Press, Honolulu.

Klor de Alva, J. Jorge

1996   Mestizaje from New Spain to Aztlán: On the Control and Classification of Collective Identities. In *New World Orders: Casta Paintings and Colonial Latin America,* edited by Ilona Katzew, pp. 78–51. Americas Society, New York.

Lapham, Heather

2001   More than "A Few Blew Beads": The Glass and Stone Beads from Jamestown Rediscovery's 1994–1997 Excavations. *The Journal of the Jamestown Rediscovery Center* 1. Electronic document, http://www.apva.org/resource/jjrc/vo11/index.html, accessed November 21, 2008.

Larsen, Clark Spencer, Mark C. Griffin, Dale L. Hutchinson, Vivian E. Noble, Lynette Norr, Robert F. Pastor, Christopher B. Ruff, Katherine F. Russell, Margaret J. Schoeninger, Michael Schultz, Scott W. Simpson, and Mark F. Teaford

2001   Frontiers of Contact: Bioarchaeology in Spanish Florida. *Journal of World Prehistory* 15(1):69–123.

Le Moyne de Morgues, Jacques

1875   *Narrative of Le Moyne, an Artist who Accompanied the French Expedition to Florida under Laudonniere, 1564.* Translated from the Latin of De Bry, with heliotypes of the engravings taken from the artist's original drawings. JR Osgood and Company, Boston.

Le Page du Pratz, A. S.

1975   *The History of Louisiana.* English reprint of the 1774 original edition, Louisiana American Revolution Bicentennial Commission. Louisiana State University Press, Baton Rouge.

Le Petit, Father

1730   Letter from Father le Petit, Missionary, to Father d'Avaugour, Procurator of the Missions in North America, July 12, 1730. In *The Jesuit Relations and*

Allied Documents, Vol. 68, edited by Reuben Gold Thwaites, pp. 119–223. Pageant Book Co., New York.

Lepore, Jill

1998 *The Name of War: King Philip's War and the Origins of American Identity.* Knopf, New York.

Lexington Historical Society

2007 Hancock-Clarke House. Electronic document, http://www.lexingtonhistory.org/pmwiki.php?n=Main.Hancock-ClarkeHouse, accessed December 4, 2008.

Liebmann, Matthew J.

2002 Signs of Power and Resistance: The (Re)Creation of Christian Imagery and Identities in the Pueblo Revolt Era. In *Archaeologies of the Pueblo Revolt: Identity, Meaning, and Renewal in the Pueblo World,* edited by Robert W. Pruecel, pp. 132–143. University of New Mexico Press, Albuquerque.

Lightfoot, Kent G.

1995 Culture Contact Studies: Redefining the Relationship between Prehistoric and Historical Archaeology. *American Antiquity* 60(2):199–217.

2004 *Indians, Missionaries, and Merchants: The Legacy of Colonial Encounters on the California Frontiers.* University of California Press, Berkeley.

Lindauer, Owen

1996 *Historical Archaeology of the United States Industrial Indian School at Phoenix: Investigation of a Turn of the Century Trash Dump.* Anthropological Field Studies 42. Office of Cultural Resource Management, Department of Anthropology, Arizona State University, Tempe.

1997 *Not for School, but for Life: Lessons from the Historical Archaeology of the Phoenix Indian School.* Office of Cultural Resources Management Report 95. Office of Cultural Resource Management, Department of Anthropology, Arizona State University, Tempe.

Lindman, Janet Moore, and Michele Lise Tarter

2001 "The earthly frame, a minute Fabrick, a Centre of Wonders." In *A Centre of Wonders: The Body in Early America,* edited by Janet M. Lindman and Michele L. Tarter, pp. 1–9. Cornell University Press, Ithaca, New York.

Little, Barbara J.

1992 *Text-Aided Archaeology.* CRC Press, Boca Raton, Florida.

Little, Ann M.

2001 "Shoot That Rogue, for He Hath an Englishman's Coat On!": Cultural Cross-Dressing on the New England Frontier, 1620–1760. *The New England Quarterly* 74(2):238–273.

Loren, Diana DiPaolo

2001a Manipulating Bodies and Emerging Traditions at the Los Adaes Presidio. In *The Archaeology of Traditions: Agency and History before and after Colum-*

bus, edited by Timothy R. Pauketat, pp. 58–76. University of Florida Press, Gainesville.

2001b Social Skins: Orthodoxies and Practices of Dressing in the Early Colonial Lower Mississippi Valley. *Journal of Social Archaeology* 1(2):172–189.

2004 Creolization in the French and Spanish Colonies. In *North American Archaeology,* edited by Timothy R. Pauketat and Diana DiPaolo Loren, pp. 297–318. Blackwell Press, Oxford.

2007a *In Contact: Bodies and Landscapes in the 16th and 17th-Century Eastern Woodlands.* Altamira Press, Walnut Creek, California.

2007b Corporeal Concerns: Eighteenth-Century Casta Paintings and Colonial Bodies in Spanish Texas. *Historical Archaeology* 41(1):23–36.

Loren, Diana DiPaolo, and Uzi Baram

2007 Between Art and Artifact: Approaches to Visual Representations in Historical Archaeology. *Historical Archaeology* 41(1):1–5.

Loren, Diana DiPaolo, and Mary C. Beaudry

2006 Becoming American: Small Things Remembered. In *Historical Archaeology,* edited by Stephen W. Silliman and Martin Hall, pp. 251–271. Blackwell Press, Oxford.

Luckenbach, Al, and C. Jane Cox

2003 17th Century Lead Cloth Seals from Anne Arundel County, Maryland. *Maryland Archaeology* 39(1–2).

Lurie, Alison

2000 *The Language of Clothes.* Henry Holt and Company, New York.

Malischke, LisaMarie

2009 *The Excavated Bead Collection at Fort St. Joseph (20BE23) and Its Implication for Understanding Adornment, Ideology, Cultural Exchange and Identity.* Master's thesis, Department of Anthropology, Western Michigan University, Kalamazoo, Michigan.

Mallios, Seth

2000 *At the Edge of the Precipice: Frontier Ventures, Jamestown's Hinterland, and the Archaeology of 44JC802.* Association for the Preservation of Virginia Antiquities, Richmond, Virginia.

Mann, Rob B.

2007 "True Portraitures of the Indians, and of Their Own Peculiar Conceits of Dress": Discourses of Dress and Identity in the Great Lakes, 1830–1850. *Historical Archaeology* 41(1):37–52.

Mann, Rob B., and Diana DiPaolo Loren

2001 Keeping Up Appearances: Dress, Architecture, Furniture, and Status at French Azilum. *International Journal of Historical Archaeology* 5(4):281–307.

Maryland Archaeological Conservation Lab

2007 A Comparative Archaeological Study of Colonial Chesapeake Culture. Electronic document, http://www.chesapeakearchaeology.org/Index.htm, accessed July 11, 2008.

Mays, Dorothy A.

2004 *Women in Early America: Struggle, Survival, and Freedom in a New World.* ABC-CLIO, Santa Barbara, California.

McBride, Bunny

2001 *Women of the Dawn.* University of Nebraska Press, Omaha.

McEwan, Bonnie G.

1993 *The Spanish Missions of La Florida.* University of Florida Press, Gainesville.

2001 The Spiritual Conquest of La Florida. *American Anthropologist* 103(3): 633–644.

Merleau-Ponty, Maurice

1989 *Phenomenology of Perception.* Routledge, London.

Meskell, Lynn

2002 The Intersections of Identity and Politics in Archaeology. *Annual Review of Anthropology* 31:279–301.

2004 *Object Worlds in Ancient Egypt: Material Biographies Past and Present.* Blackwell Press, Oxford.

Miller, Daniel

2005 *Materiality.* Duke University Press, Durham, North Carolina.

Mobley-Tanaka, Jeannette L.

2002 Crossed Cultures, Crossed Meanings: The Manipulation of Ritual Imagery on the Early Historic Pueblo Resistance. In *Archaeologies of the Pueblo Revolt: Identity, Meaning, and Renewal in the Pueblo World,* edited by Robert W. Pruecel, pp. 77–98. University of New Mexico Press, Albuquerque.

Morand, Lynn L.

1994 *Craft Industries at Fort Michilimackinac, 1715–1781.* Archaeological Completion Report Series, No. 15. Mackinac State Historic Parks, Mackinac Island, Michigan.

Morgan, Gwenda, and Peter Rushton

2005 Visible Bodies: Power, Subordination and Identity in the Eighteenth-Century Atlantic World. *Journal of Social History* 39(1):39–64.

Morison, Samuel Eliot

1995 *The Founding of Harvard College.* Harvard University Press, Cambridge, Massachusetts.

Moser, Stephanie

1998 *Ancestral Images: The Iconography of Human Origins.* Cornell University Press, Ithaca, New York.

Munns, Jessica, and Penny Richards
1999   *The Clothes That Wear Us: Essays on Dressing and Transgressing in Eighteenth-Century Culture.* University of Delaware Press, Newark.
Nassaney, Michael S.
2004   Native American Gender Politics and Material Culture in Seventeenth-Century Southeastern New England. *Journal of Social Archaeology* 4(3):334–367.
2005   Men and Women, Pipes and Power in Native New England. In *Smoking and Culture: The Archaeology of Tobacco Pipes in Eastern North America,* edited by Sean M. Rafferty and Rob Mann, pp. 125–141. University of Tennessee Press, Knoxville.
2008   Identity Formation at a French Colonial Outpost in the North American Interior. *International Journal of Historical Archaeology* 12(4):297–318
Nassaney, Michael S., and Eric S. Johnson
2000   The Contributions of Material Objects to Ethnohistory in Native North America. In *Interpretations of Native North American Life: Material Contributions to Ethnohistory,* edited by M. S. Nassaney and E. S. Johnson, pp. 1–30. University Press of Florida, Gainesville.
National Park Service
2008   Grand Village of the Natchez Indians. Electronic document, http://www.nps.gov/history/NR/travel/mounds/gra.htm, accessed June 5, 2008.
Neill, Susan M.
2000   Emblems of Ethnicity: Ribbonwork Garments from the Great Lakes Region. In *Interpretations of Native North American Life: Material Contributions to Ethnohistory,* edited by M. S. Nassaney and E. S. Johnson, pp. 146–170. University Press of Florida, Gainesville.
Neitzel, Robert S.
1965   *Archaeology of the Fatherland Site: The Grand Village of the Natchez,* Vol. 51, Pt. 1. Anthropological Papers of the American Museum of Natural History, New York.
1983   *The Grand Village of the Natchez Revisited: Excavations of the Fatherland Site, Adams County, Mississippi, 1972,* Archaeological Report No. 12, Mississippi Department of Archives and History, Jackson.
Noël Hume, Audrey
1973   *Five Artifact Studies.* Colonial Williamsburg Foundation, distributed by University Press of Virginia, Charlottesville.
Noël Hume, Ivor
1969   *A Guide to Artifacts of Colonial America.* University of Pennsylvania Press, Philadelphia.
Noël Hume, Ivor, and Audrey Noël Hume
2001   *The Archaeology of Martin's Hundred,* Pt. I, *Interpretive Studies.* The Colonial Williamsburg Foundation, Williamsburg, Virginia.

Ordonez, Margaret T., and Linda Welters
1998   Textiles from the Seventeenth-Century Privy at the Cross Street Back Lot
        Site. *Historical Archaeology* 32(3):81–90.
Orser, Charles E.
2007   *The Archaeology of Race and Racialization in Historic America.* University of
        Florida Press, Gaineseville.
Pagden, Anthony
1982   *The Fall of Natural Man: The American Indian and the Origins of Comparative
        Ethnology.* Cambridge University Press, Cambridge.
Parker Pearson, Michael
1999   *Archaeology of Death and Burial.* Texas A&M University Press, College Park,
        Texas.
Phillips, Ruth B.
1998   *Trading Identities: The Souvenir in Native North American Art from the
        Northeast, 1700–1900.* University of Washington Press, Seattle.
Pietak, Lynn Marie
1998   Body Symbolism and Cultural Aesthetics: The Use of Shell Beads and Or-
        naments by Delaware and Munsee Groups. *North American Archaeologist*
        19(2):135–161.
Pinney, Christopher
1997   *Camera Indica: The Social Life of Indian photographs.* University of Chicago
        Press, Chicago.
Pruecel, Robert W.
2002   Writing the Pueblo Revolt. In *Archaeologies of the Pueblo Revolt: Identity,
        Meaning, and Renewal in the Pueblo World,* edited by Robert W. Pruecel, pp.
        3–32. University of New Mexico Press, Albuquerque.
Pruecel, Robert W., and Lynn Meskell
2004   Knowledges. In *A Companion to Social Archaeology,* edited by Lynn Meskell
        and Robert W. Pruecel, pp. 3–22. Blackwell Publishers, Oxford.
Quimby, George I.
1966   *Indian Culture and European Trade Goods.* University of Wisconsin Press,
        Madison.
Reddy, William M.
1988   The Structure of a Cultural Crisis: Thinking about Cloth in France before
        and after the Revolution. In *The Social Life of Things: Commodities in Cultur-
        al Perspective,* edited by Arjun Appaduri, pp. 361–384. Cambridge University
        Press, Cambridge.
Richardson, Catherine (editor)
2004   *Clothing Culture, 1350–1650: The History of Retailing and Consumption.* Ash-
        gate Publishers, Burlington, Vermont.

Richardson, Jane, and Alfred L. Kroeber

1952   "Three Centuries of Women's Dress Fashions: A Quantitative Analysis." In *The Nature of Culture,* edited by Alfred L. Kroeber, pp. 318–372. University of Chicago Press, Chicago.

Roach, Mary Ellen, and Joanne B. Eicher

1965   *Dress, Adornment, and the Social Order.* John Wiley & Sons, New York.

1973   *The Visible Self: Perspectives on Dress.* Prentice Hall, New York.

Roche, Daniel

1994   *The Culture of Clothing: Dress and Fashion in the 'Ancien Régime.'* Cambridge University Press, Cambridge.

Rothschild, Nan A.

1996   Social Distance between Dutch Settlers and Native Americans. In *One Man's Trash Is Another Man's Treasure,* edited by Alexandra van Dongen, pp. 189–201. Museum Boymans-van Beuningen, Rotterdam.

2003   *Colonial Encounters in a Native American Landscape: The Spanish and Dutch in North America.* Smithsonian Institution Press, Washington, D.C.

Rowland, Dunbar, and A. G. Sanders (translators and editors)

1929   *Mississippi Provincial Archives, French Dominion.* Vol. 2, *1701–1729.* Mississippi Department of Archives and History, Jackson.

Sayre, Gordon M.

1997   *Les Sauvages Américains: Representations of Native Americans in French and English Colonial Literature.* University of North Carolina Press, Chapel Hill.

Scarre, Chris, and Geoffrey Scarre (editors)

2006   *The Ethics of Archaeology: Philosophical Perspectives on Archaeological Practice.* Cambridge University Press, Cambridge.

Schneider, Jane

2006   Cloth and Clothing. In *Handbook of Material Culture,* edited by Chris Tilley, Webb Keane, Susanne Küchler, Mike Rowlands, and Patricia Spyer, pp. 203–220. Sage Publications, London.

Sempowski, Martha L.

1994   Early Historic Exchange between the Seneca and the Susquehannock. In *Proceedings of the 1992 People to People Conference,* edited by Charles F. Hayes, pp. 51–64. Research Records 23, Rochester Museum and Science Center, Rochester.

Shannon, Timothy J.

1996   Dressing for Success on the Mohawk Frontier: Hendrick, William Johnson, and the Indian Fashion. *William and Mary Quarterly,* 3rd ser., 53(1):13–42.

Silliman, Stephen

2001   Agency, Practical Politics, and the Archaeology of Culture Contact. *Journal of Social Archaeology* 1(2):190–209.

2005   Culture Contact or Colonialism? Challenges in the Archaeology of Native North America. *American Antiquity* 70(1):55–74.

Silverman, David J.

2005   *Faith and Boundaries: Colonists, Christianity, and Community among the Wampanoag Indians of Martha's Vineyard, 1600–1871.* Cambridge University Press, Cambridge.

Singleton, Theresa

2005   Before the Revolution: Archaeology and the African Diaspora on the Atlantic Seaboard. In *North American Archaeology,* edited by Timothy R. Pauketat and Diana DiPaolo Loren, pp. 297–318. Blackwell Press, Oxford.

Smith, Claire, and H. Martin Wobst

2005   *Indigenous Archaeologies: Decolonizing Theory and Practice.* Routledge Press, London.

Smith, Ira F., and Jeffrey R. Graybill

1977   A Report on the Shenks Ferry and Susquehannock Components at the Funk Site, Lancaster County, Pennsylvania. *Man in the Northeast* 13:45–65.

Smith, John

1624   *The Generall Historie of Virginia, New England & the Summer Isles.* I. D. and I. H. for Michael Sparkes, London.

Sokolow, Jayme A.

2003   *The Great Encounter: Native Peoples and European Settlers in the Americas, 1492–1800.* M. E. Sharpe Publishers, Armonk, New York.

South, Stanley

1977   *Method and Theory in Historical Archaeology.* Academic Press, New York.

Spear, Jennifer M.

1999   "They Need Wives": Métissage and the Regulation of Sexuality in French Louisiana, 1699–1730. In *Sex, Love, Race: Crossing Boundaries in North American History,* edited by Martha Hodes, pp. 35–59. New York University Press, New York.

2003   Colonial Intimacies: Legislating Sex in French Louisiana. *William and Mary Quarterly* 3rd ser., 60(1):75–98.

St. George, Robert Blair

1998   *Conversing by Signs: Poetics of Implication in Colonial New England Culture.* University of North Carolina Press, Winston-Salem.

2000   Introduction. In *Possible Pasts: Becoming Colonial in Early America,* edited by Robert Blair St. George, pp. 1–32. Cornell University Press, Ithaca, New York.

Stahl, Ann Brower

1993   Concepts of Time and Approaches to Analogical Reasoning in the Historical Perspective. *American Antiquity* 58(2):235–260.

2001   Colonial Entanglements and the Practices of Taste: An Alternative to Logo-centric Approaches. *American Anthropologist* 104(3):827–845.

Steiner, Chris

1990   Body Personal and Body Public: Adornment and Leadership in Cross-Cultural Perspective. *Anthropos* 85:431–445.

Stephens, Sarah

2010   *Posh Priests or Modest Ministers: A Study of Personal Adornment at the Hancock-Clarke House, Lexington, MA.* Master's thesis, Department of Anthropology, University of Massachusetts Boston.

Stoler, Ann Laura

1997   Sexual Affronts and Racial Frontiers: European Identities and the Politics of Exclusion in Colonial Southeast Asia. In *Tensions of Empire: Colonial Cultures in a Bourgeois World,* edited by Frederick Cooper and Ann Laura Stoler, pp. 198–237. University of California Press, Berkeley.

2001   Tense and Tender Ties: The Politics of Comparison in North American History and Colonial Studies. *The Journal of American History* 88(3):829–865.

Stubbs, John D.

1992   *Underground Harvard: The Archaeology of College Life.* Ph.D. dissertation, Department of Anthropology, Harvard University.

Swanton, John R.

1911   *Indian Tribes of the Lower Mississippi Valley and Adjacent Coast of Mexico.* Bureau of American Ethnology Bulletin 43. Smithsonian Institution, Washington, D.C.

Thomas, Brian W.

2002   Struggling with the Past: Some Views of African American Identity. *International Journal of Historical Archaeology* 6(2):143–151.

Thomas, David Hurst

1993   The Archaeology of Mission Santa Catalina de Guale: Our First 15 Years. In *The Spanish Missions of La Florida,* edited by Bonnie G. McEwan, pp. 1–34. University Press of Florida, Gainesville.

Thomas, Nicholas

1991   *Entangled Objects: Exchange, Material Culture and Colonialism in the Pacific.* Harvard University Press, Cambridge, Massachusetts.

Thomas, Nicholas, Anna Cole, and Bronwen Douglas

2005   *Tattoo: Bodies, Art, and Exchange in the Pacific and the West.* Duke University Press, Durham, North Carolina.

Treherne, P.

1995   The Warrior's Beauty: The Masculine Body and Self-Identity in Bronze-Age Europe. *Journal of European Archaeology* 3(1):105–144.

Turgeon, Laurier

2001   French Beads in France and Northeastern North America during the Six-
        teenth Century. *Historical Archaeology* 35(4):58–82.

2004   Beads, Bodies and Regimes of Value: From France to North America, c.
        1500–c. 1650. In *The Archaeology of Contact in Settler Societies*, edited by
        Tim Murray, pp. 19–47. Cambridge University Press, Cambridge.

2006   The Cartier Voyages to Canada (1534–1542) and the Beginnings of French
        Colonialism in North America. In *Charting Change: in France around 1540*,
        edited by Marian Rothstein, pp. 97–118. Susquehanna University Press, Se-
        linsgrove, Pennsylvania.

Turner, T.

1993 [1980]   The social skin. In *Reading the Social Body*, edited by C.B. Burroughs
        and J. Ehrenreich, pp. 15–39. University of Iowa Press, Iowa City.

Ulrich, Laurel Thatcher

2001   *The Age of Homespun: Objects and Stories in the Creation of an American
        Myth*. Alfred A. Knopf, New York.

1991   Cloth, Clothing and Early American Social History. *Dress* 18:39–48.

Usner, D. H.

1992   *Indians, Settlers and Slaves in a Frontier Exchange Economy: The Lower Mis-
        sissippi Valley before 1783*. University of North Carolina Press, Chapel Hill.

Veit, Richard

2002   *Digging New Jersey's Past: Historical Archaeology in the Garden State*. Rutgers
        University Press New Brunswick, New Jersey.

Veit, Richard, and Charles A. Bello.

1999   "A unique and valuable historical and Indian collection": Charles Conrad
        Abbott Explores a Seventeenth-Century Dutch Trading Post in the Delaware
        Valley. *Journal of Middle Atlantic Archaeology* 15:95–123.

Vitelli, Karen D., and Chip Colwell-Chanthaphonh (editors)

2006   *Archaeological Ethics*. Altamira Press, Walnut Creek, California.

Volo, James M., and Dorothy Denneen Volo

2002   *Daily Life on the Old Colonial Frontier*. Greenwood Publishing Group, West-
        port, Connecticut.

Voss, Barbara L.

2008a   *Race, Sexuality, and Identity in Colonial San Francisco: The Archaeology of
        Ethnogenesis*. University of California Press, Berkeley.

2008b   "Poor people in silk shirts": Dress and ethnogenesis in Spanish-colonial San
        Francisco. *Journal of Social Archaeology* 8(3):404–432.

Wagner, Mark J.

1998   Cultural Change and Continuity among the Early Nineteenth-century Potawatomi. In *Studies in Culture Contact*, edited by J. Cusick, pp. 430–451. Southern Illinois University Press, Carbondale, Illinois.

Waselkov, Gregory A.

1992   French Colonial Creek Trade in the Upper Creek Country. In *Calumet and Fleur-de-Lys: Archaeology of Indian and French Contact in the Midcontinent*, edited by John A. Walthall and Thomas E. Emerson, pp. 35–53. Smithsonian Institution Press, Washington, D.C.

Waselkov, Gregory A., and Bonnie L. Gums

2000   *Plantation Archaeology at Rivière Aux Chiens, ca., 1725–1848.* University of South Alabama, Center for Archaeological Studies, Mobile, Alabama.

Watkins, Joe

2005   Representing and Repatriating the Past. In *North American Archaeology*, edited by Timothy R. Pauketat and Diana DiPaolo Loren, pp. 337–358. Blackwell Press, Oxford.

Weber, David J.

1994   *The Spanish Frontier in North America.* Yale University Press, New Haven, Connecticut.

Weiner, A.

1985   Inalienable Wealth. *American Ethnologist* 12(2):210–217.

Weiner, A., and J. Schneider (editors)

1989   *Cloth and Human Experience.* Smithsonian Institution Press, Washington, D.C.

Welters, Linda, Margaret T. Ordoñez, Kathryn Tarleton, and Joyce Smith

1985   European Textiles from Seventeenth-Century New England Cemeteries. In *Historical Archaeology and the Study of American Culture*, edited by LuAnn DeCunzo and Bernard L. Herman, pp. 193–232. Henry Francis du Pont Winterthur Museum, Winterthur, Delaware.

White, Carolyn L.

2005   *American Artifacts of Personal Adornment, 1680–1820: A Guide to Identification and Interpretation.* Altamira Press, Walnut Creek, California.

White, Carolyn L., and Mary C. Beaudry

2009   Artifacts and Personal Identity. In *International Handbook of Historical Archaeology*, edited by David Gaimster and Teresita Majewski, pp. 209–226. Springer Press, New York.

Wilcox, Michael V.

2002   Social Memory and the Pueblo Revolt: A Postcolonial Perspective. In *Archaeologies of the Pueblo Revolt: Identity, Meaning, and Renewal in the Pueblo World*, edited by Robert W. Preucel, pp. 167–179. University of New Mexico Press, Albuquerque.

Wilkie, Laurie A.

1995　Magic and Empowerment on the Plantation: An Archaeological Consideration of African-American Worldview. *Southeastern Archaeology* 14(2):136–157.

1997　Secret and Sacred: Contextualizing the Artifacts of African-American Magic and Religion. *Historical Archaeology* 31(4):81–106

Willoughby, Charles C.

1935　*Antiquities of the New England Indians with Notes on the Ancient Cultures of the Adjacent Territory.* Peabody Museum of Archaeology and Ethnology, Harvard University, Cambridge, Massachusetts.

Wolf, Eric R.

1982　*Europe and the People without History.* University of California Press, Berkeley.

Wood, W. Raymond

1990　Ethnohistory and the Historical Method. In *Archaeological Method and Theory,* Vol. 2, edited by Michael B. Schiffer, pp. 81–110. University of Arizona Press, Tucson.

Wray, Charles F.

1983　Seneca Glass Trade Beads c. A.D. 1550–1820. In *Proceedings of the 1982 Glass Bead Conference*, edited by Charles F. Hayes, pp. 41–49, Research Records No. 16, Rochester Museum and Science Division, Rochester, New York.

Wray, Charles F., Martha L. Sempowski, and Lorraine P. Saunders

1991　*Tram and Cameron: Two Early Contact Era Sites.* Research Records No. 21, Rochester Museum and Science Center, Rochester, New York.

Yentsch, Anne E.

1994　*A Chesapeake Family and Their Slaves: A Study in Historical Archaeology.* Cambridge University Press, Cambridge.

Zierden, Martha

2002　Frontier Society in South Carolina: An Example from Willtown (1690–1800). In *Another's Country: Archaeological and Historical Perspectives on Cultural Interactions in the Southern Colonies,* edited by J. W. Joseph and Martha Zierden, pp. 181–197. University of Alabama Press, Tuscaloosa.

Zimmerman, Larry J., Karen D. Vitelli, and Julie Hollowell-Zimmer (editors)

2003　*Ethical Issues in Archaeology.* Altamira Press, Walnut Creek, California.

Index

Page numbers in italics refer to illustrations.

Diana DiPaolo Loren has been an associate curator at the Peabody Museum of Archaeology and Ethnology, Harvard University, since 1999. Loren is a North American archaeologist specializing on the colonial period Southeast and Northeast. Her research interests include colonialism, identity, social theories of the body, and artifacts of clothing and adornment. She is the author of *In Contact: Bodies and Spaces in the Sixteenth- and Seventeenth-Century Eastern Woodlands* and co-editor of *North American Archaeology* with Timothy R. Pauketat.

www.ingramcontent.com/pod-product-compliance
Lightning Source LLC
Chambersburg PA
CBHW021338090426
42742CB00008B/656